International
Coordination of
National Stabilization
Policies

Integrating National Economies: Promise and Pitfalls

Barry Bosworth (Brookings Institution) and Gur Ofer (Hebrew University)
Reforming Planned Economies in an Integrating World Economy

Ralph C. Bryant (Brookings Institution)
International Coordination of National Stabilization Policies

Susan M. Collins (Brookings Institution/Georgetown University)
Distributive Issues: A Constraint on Global Integration

Richard N. Cooper (Harvard University)
Environment and Resource Policies for the World Economy

Ronald G. Ehrenberg (Cornell University)
Labor Markets and Integrating National Economies

Barry Eichengreen (University of California, Berkeley)
International Monetary Arrangements for the 21st Century

Mitsuhiro Fukao (Bank of Japan)
Financial Integration, Corporate Governance, and the Performance of Multinational Companies

Stephan Haggard (University of California, San Diego)
Developing Nations and the Politics of Global Integration

Richard J. Herring (University of Pennsylvania) and Robert E. Litan (Department of Justice/Brookings Institution)
Financial Regulation in the Global Economy

Miles Kahler (University of California, San Diego)
International Institutions and the Political Economy of Integration

Anne O. Krueger (Stanford University)
Trade Policies and Developing Nations

Robert Z. Lawrence (Harvard University)
Regionalism, Multilateralism, and Deeper Integration

Sylvia Ostry (University of Toronto) and Richard R. Nelson (Columbia University)
Techno-Nationalism and Techno-Globalism: Conflict and Cooperation

Robert L. Paarlberg (Wellesley College/Harvard University)
Leadership Abroad Begins at Home: U.S. Foreign Economic Policy after the Cold War

Peter Rutland (Wesleyan University)
Russia, Eurasia, and the Global Economy

F. M. Scherer (Harvard University)
Competition Policies for an Integrated World Economy

Susan L. Shirk (University of California, San Diego)
How China Opened Its Door: The Political Success of the PRC's Foreign Trade and Investment Reforms

Alan O. Sykes (University of Chicago)
Product Standards for Internationally Integrated Goods Markets

Akihiko Tanaka (Institute of Oriental Culture, University of Tokyo)
The Politics of Deeper Integration: National Attitudes and Policies in Japan

Vito Tanzi (International Monetary Fund)
Taxation in an Integrating World

William Wallace (St. Antony's College, Oxford University)
Regional Integration: The West European Experience

Ralph C. Bryant

International Coordination of National Stabilization Policies

THE BROOKINGS INSTITUTION
Washington, D.C.

Copyright © 1995
THE BROOKINGS INSTITUTION
1775 Massachusetts Avenue, N. W., Washington, D.C. 20036

Library of Congress Cataloging-in-Publication data:
Bryant, Ralph C., 1938–
International coordination of national stabilization policies/
Ralph C. Bryant.
p. cm.—(Integrating national economies: promise and pitfalls)
Includes bibliographical references and index.
ISBN 0-8157-1256-1 (alk. paper).—ISBN 0-8157-1255-3 (pbk. : alk. paper)
1. International economic integration.   2. Economic stabilization.
3. Economic policy.   I. Title.   II. Series: Integrating national economies.
HF1418.5.B79   1995
339.5—dc20   95-21563
                                                                CIP

9 8 7 6 5 4 3 2 1

The paper used in this publication meets the minimum requirements of
American National Standard for Information Sciences—Permanence of Paper
for Printed Library Materials, ANSI Z39.48-1984

Typeset in Plantin

Composition by Princeton Editorial Associates
Princeton, New Jersey

Printed by R. R. Donnelley and Sons Co.
Harrisonburg, Virginia

Foreword

*F*OR THE foreseeable future the world will continue to be organized politically into nation-states with sovereign governments. Yet in the second half of the twentieth century the economic links among nations have been growing more rapidly than economic activity itself. As economic integration increases, the differences among national economies have eroded, and the policy autonomy of national governments has been undermined.

Because economic integration intensifies the cross-border spillovers among national economies and makes national policymaking more difficult, the possibility arises that national governments may all be able to benefit by coordinating their decisions about macroeconomic stabilization policies. But would the gains be significant? And if national governments decide to cooperate in setting policies, how ambitiously should they try to do so? In his contribution to the Brookings series of books on Integrating National Economies Ralph C. Bryant addresses these issues, posed by international cooperation and coordination, that stem from the growing tension between national political sovereignty and economic integration.

An earlier essay drawn from Bryant's research on this subject was presented at a conference in April 1993 at Princeton University, held to commemorate the fiftieth anniversary of the Princeton International Finance Section's series of *Essays in International Finance.* That essay was published in Peter B. Kenen, ed., *Understanding Interdependence: The Macroeconomics of the Open Economy* (Princeton University Press, 1995). This book greatly revises and expands that earlier paper.

Bryant is a senior fellow in the Brookings Economic Studies program. He is grateful for the help of many colleagues and friends during the course of his research and writing. A preliminary version of his manuscript was discussed at a review conference by Paul R. Masson and Takatoshi Ito. Bryant was able to improve the final manuscript significantly by taking into account Masson's and Ito's insightful comments. Henry Aaron, Stanley Black, Benjamin J. Cohen, Susan Collins, Richard Cooper, Max Corden, Barry Eichengreen, Mitsuhiro Fukao, Morris Goldstein, Dale Henderson, Andrew Hughes Hallett, Peter Kenen, Robert Lawrence, Warwick McKibbin, Robert Paarlberg, Robert Solomon, and Edwin Truman made other helpful comments or suggestions. Gianluca Bacchiocchi and Long Zhang contributed able research assistance.

Theresa Walker shepherded the manuscript through the publication process, Jeffrey McConnell verified the factual content, and Princeton Editorial Associates prepared the index. Evelyn Taylor provided administrative assistance.

Funding for the project came from the Center for Global Partnership of the Japan Foundation, the Curry Foundation, the Ford Foundation, the Korea Foundation, the Tokyo Club Foundation for Global Studies, the United States-Japan Foundation, and the Alex C. Walker Educational and Charitable Foundation. The author and Brookings are grateful for their support.

BRUCE K. MACLAURY
President

August 1995
Washington, D.C.

Contents

Figures

Preface to the Studies on Integrating National Economies

*E*CONOMIC interdependence among nations has increased sharply in the past half century. For example, while the value of total production of industrial countries increased at a rate of about 9 percent a year on average between 1964 and 1992, the value of the exports of those nations grew at an average rate of 12 percent, and lending and borrowing across national borders through banks surged upward even more rapidly at 23 percent a year. This international economic interdependence has contributed to significantly improved standards of living for most countries. Continuing international economic integration holds out the promise of further benefits. Yet the increasing sensitivity of national economies to events and policies originating abroad creates dilemmas and pitfalls if national policies and international cooperation are poorly managed.

The Brookings Project on Integrating National Economies, of which this study is a component, focuses on the interplay between two fundamental facts about the world at the end of the twentieth century. First, the world will continue for the foreseeable future to be organized politically into nation-states with sovereign governments. Second, increasing economic integration among nations will continue to erode differences among national economies and undermine the autonomy of national governments. The project explores the opportunities and tensions arising from these two facts.

Scholars from a variety of disciplines have produced twenty-one studies for the first phase of the project. Each study examines the heightened competition between national political sovereignty and increased cross-border economic integration. This preface identifies background themes and issues common to all the studies and provides a brief overview of the project as a whole.[1]

Increasing World Economic Integration

Two underlying sets of causes have led nations to become more closely intertwined. First, technological, social, and cultural changes have sharply reduced the effective economic distances among nations. Second, many of the government policies that traditionally inhibited cross-border transactions have been relaxed or even dismantled.

The same improvements in transportation and communications technology that make it much easier and cheaper for companies in New York to ship goods to California, for residents of Strasbourg to visit relatives in Marseilles, and for investors in Hokkaido to buy and sell shares on the Tokyo Stock Exchange facilitate trade, migration, and capital movements spanning nations and continents. The sharply reduced costs of moving goods, money, people, and information underlie the profound economic truth that technology has made the world markedly smaller.

New communications technology has been especially significant for financial activity. Computers, switching devices, and telecommunications satellites have slashed the cost of transmitting information internationally, of confirming transactions, and of paying for transactions. In the 1950s, for example, foreign exchange could be bought and sold only during conventional business hours in the initiating party's time zone. Such transactions can now be carried out instantaneously twenty-four hours a day. Large banks pass the management of their worldwide foreign-exchange positions around the globe from one branch to another, staying continuously ahead of the setting sun.

Such technological innovations have increased the knowledge of potentially profitable international exchanges and of economic opportunities abroad. Those developments, in turn, have changed consumers' and producers' tastes. Foreign goods, foreign vacations, foreign financial investments—virtually anything from other nations—have lost some of their exotic character.

---

1. A complete list of authors and study titles is included at the beginning of this volume, facing the title page.

Although technological change permits increased contact among nations, it would not have produced such dramatic effects if it had been countermanded by government policies. Governments have traditionally taxed goods moving in international trade, directly restricted imports and subsidized exports, and tried to limit international capital movements. Those policies erected "separation fences" at the borders of nations. From the perspective of private sector agents, separation fences imposed extra costs on cross-border transactions. They reduced trade and, in some cases, eliminated it. During the 1930s governments used such policies with particular zeal, a practice now believed to have deepened and lengthened the Great Depression.

After World War II, most national governments began—sometimes unilaterally, more often collaboratively—to lower their separation fences, to make them more permeable, or sometimes even to tear down parts of them. The multilateral negotiations under the auspices of the General Agreement on Trade and Tariffs (GATT)—for example, the Kennedy Round in the 1960s, the Tokyo Round in the 1970s, and most recently the protracted negotiations of the Uruguay Round, formally signed only in April 1994—stand out as the most prominent examples of fence lowering for trade in goods. Though contentious and marked by many compromises, the GATT negotiations are responsible for sharp reductions in at-the-border restrictions on trade in goods and services. After the mid-1980s a large number of developing countries moved unilaterally to reduce border barriers and to pursue outwardly oriented policies.

The lowering of fences for financial transactions began later and was less dramatic. Nonetheless, by the 1990s government restrictions on capital flows, especially among the industrial countries, were much less important and widespread than at the end of World War II and in the 1950s.

By shrinking the economic distances among nations, changes in technology would have progressively integrated the world economy even in the absence of reductions in governments' separation fences. Reductions in separation fences would have enhanced interdependence even without the technological innovations. Together, these two sets of evolutionary changes have reinforced each other and strikingly transformed the world economy.

Changes in the Government of Nations

Simultaneously with the transformation of the global economy, major changes have occurred in the world's political structure. First, the number of governmental decisionmaking units in the world has expanded markedly, and political power has been diffused more broadly among them. Rising nationalism and, in some areas, heightened ethnic tensions have accompanied that increasing political pluralism.

The history of membership in international organizations documents the sharp growth in the number of independent states. For example, only 44 nations participated in the Bretton Woods conference of July 1944, which gave birth to the International Monetary Fund. But by the end of 1970, the IMF had 118 member nations. The number of members grew to 150 by the mid-1980s and to 178 by December 1993. Much of this growth reflects the collapse of colonial empires. Although many nations today are small and carry little individual weight in the global economy, their combined influence is considerable, and their interests cannot be ignored as easily as they were in the past.

A second political trend, less visible but equally important, has been the gradual loss of the political and economic hegemony of the United States. Immediately after World War II, the United States by itself accounted for more than one-third of world production. By the early 1990s the U.S. share had fallen to about one-fifth. Concurrently, the political and economic influence of the European colonial powers continued to wane, and the economic significance of nations outside Europe and North America, such as Japan, Korea, Indonesia, China, Brazil, and Mexico, increased. A world in which economic power and influence are widely diffused has displaced a world in which one or a few nations effectively dominated international decisionmaking.

Turmoil and the prospect of fundamental change in the formerly centrally planned economies compose a third factor causing radical changes in world politics. During the era of central planning, governments in those nations tried to limit external influences on their economies. Now leaders in the formerly planned economies are trying to adopt reforms modeled on Western capitalist principles. To the extent that these efforts succeed, those nations will increase their economic involvement with the rest of the world. Political and economic alignments among the Western industrialized nations will be forced to adapt.

Governments and scholars have begun to assess these three trends, but their far-reaching ramifications will not be clear for decades.

Dilemmas for National Policies

Cross-border economic integration and national political sovereignty have increasingly come into conflict, leading to a growing mismatch between the economic and political structures of the world. The effective domains of economic markets have come to coincide less and less with national governmental jurisdictions.

When the separation fences at nations' borders were high, governments and citizens could sharply distinguish "international" from "domestic" policies. International policies dealt with at-the-border barriers, such as tariffs and quotas, or responded to events occurring abroad. In contrast, domestic policies were concerned with everything behind the nation's borders, such as competition and antitrust rules, corporate governance, product standards, worker safety, regulation and supervision of financial institutions, environmental protection, tax codes, and the government's budget. Domestic policies were regarded as matters about which nations were sovereign, to be determined by the preferences of the nation's citizens and its political institutions, without regard for effects on other nations.

As separation fences have been lowered and technological innovations have shrunk economic distances, a multitude of formerly neglected differences among nations' domestic policies have become exposed to international scrutiny. National governments and international negotiations must thus increasingly deal with "deeper"—behind-the-border—integration. For example, if country A permits companies to emit air and water pollutants whereas country B does not, companies that use pollution-generating methods of production will find it cheaper to produce in country A. Companies in country B that compete internationally with companies in country A are likely to complain that foreign competitors enjoy unfair advantages and to press for international pollution standards.

Deeper integration requires analysis of the economic and the political aspects of virtually all nonborder policies and practices. Such issues have already figured prominently in negotiations over the evolution of the European Community, over the Uruguay Round of GATT negotiations, over the North American Free Trade Agreement (NAFTA), and over the bilateral economic relationships between Japan and the United States. Future debates about behind-the-border policies will occur with increasing frequency and prove at least as complex and contentious as the past negotiations regarding at-the-border restrictions.

Tensions about deeper integration arise from three broad sources: cross-border spillovers, diminished national autonomy, and challenges to political sovereignty.

Cross-Border Spillovers

Some activities in one nation produce consequences that spill across borders and affect other nations. Illustrations of these spillovers abound. Given the impact of modern technology of banking and securities markets in creating interconnected networks, lax rules in one nation erode the ability of all other nations to enforce banking and securities rules and to deal with fraudulent transactions. Given the rapid diffusion of knowledge, science and technology policies in one nation generate knowledge that other nations can use without full payment. Labor market policies become matters of concern to other nations because workers migrate in search of work; policies in one nation can trigger migration that floods or starves labor markets elsewhere. When one nation dumps pollutants into the air or water that other nations breathe or drink, the matter goes beyond the unitary concern of the polluting nation and becomes a matter for international negotiation. Indeed, the hydrocarbons that are emitted into the atmosphere when individual nations burn coal for generating electricity contribute to global warming and are thereby a matter of concern for the entire world.

The tensions associated with cross-border spillovers can be especially vexing when national policies generate outcomes alleged to be competitively inequitable, as in the example in which country A permits companies to emit pollutants and country B does not. Or consider a situation in which country C requires commodities, whether produced at home or abroad, to meet certain design standards, justified for safety reasons. Foreign competitors may find it too expensive to meet these standards. In that event, the standards in C act very much like tariffs or quotas, effectively narrowing or even eliminating foreign competition for domestic producers. Citing examples of this sort, producers or governments in individual nations often complain that business is not conducted on a "level playing field." Typically, the complaining nation proposes that *other* nations adjust their policies to moderate or remove the competitive inequities.

Arguments for creating a level playing field are troublesome at best. International trade occurs precisely because of differences among nations—in resource endowments, labor skills, and consumer tastes. Nations specialize in producing goods and services in which they are relatively most efficient. In a fundamental sense, cross-border trade is valuable because the playing field is *not* level.

When David Ricardo first developed the theory of comparative advantage, he focused on differences among nations owing to climate or technology. But Ricardo could as easily have ascribed the productive differences to differing "social climates" as to physical or technological climates. Taking all "climatic" differences as given, the theory of comparative advantage argues that free trade among nations will maximize global welfare.

Taken to its logical extreme, the notion of leveling the playing field implies that nations should become homogeneous in all major respects. But that recommendation is unrealistic and even pernicious. Suppose country A decides that it is too poor to afford the costs of a clean environment, and will thus permit the production of goods that pollute local air and water supplies. Or suppose it concludes that it cannot afford stringent protections for worker safety. Country A will then argue that it is inappropriate for other nations to impute to country A the value they themselves place on a clean environment and safety standards (just as it would be inappropriate to impute the A valuations to the environment of other nations). The core of the idea of political sovereignty is to permit national residents to order their lives and property in accord with their own preferences.

Which perspective about differences among nations in behind-the-border policies is more compelling? Is country A merely exercising its national preferences and appropriately exploiting its comparative advantage in goods that are dirty or dangerous to produce? Or does a legitimate international problem exist that justifies pressure from other nations urging country A to accept changes in its policies (thus

curbing its national sovereignty)? When national governments negoti-
ate resolutions to such questions—trying to agree whether individual
nations are legitimately exercising sovereign choices or, alternatively,
engaging in behavior that is unfair or damaging to other nations—the
dialogue is invariably contentious because the resolutions depend on
the typically complex circumstances of the international spillovers
and on the relative weights accorded to the interests of particular
individuals and particular nations.

Diminished National Autonomy

As cross-border economic integration increases, governments experience greater difficulties in trying to control events within their
borders. Those difficulties, summarized by the term *diminished autonomy*, are the second set of reasons why tensions arise from the competition between political sovereignty and economic integration.

For example, nations adjust monetary and fiscal policies to influence domestic inflation and employment. In setting these policies,
smaller countries have always been somewhat constrained by foreign
economic events and policies. Today, however, all nations are constrained, often severely. More than in the past, therefore, nations may
be better able to achieve their economic goals if they work together
collaboratively in adjusting their macroeconomic policies.

Diminished autonomy and cross-border spillovers can sometimes
be allowed to persist without explicit international cooperation to
deal with them. States in the United States adopt their own tax
systems and set policies for assistance to poor single people without
any formal cooperation or limitation. Market pressures operate to
force a degree of de facto cooperation. If one state taxes corporations
too heavily, it knows business will move elsewhere. (Those familiar
with older debates about "fiscal federalism" within the United States
and other nations will recognize the similarity between those issues
and the emerging international debates about deeper integration of
national economies.) Analogously, differences among nations in regulations, standards, policies, institutions, and even social and cultural
preferences create economic incentives for a kind of arbitrage that
erodes or eliminates the differences. Such pressures involve not only
the conventional arbitrage that exploits price differentials (buying at
one point in geographic space or time and selling at another) but also

shifts in the location of production facilities and in the residence of factors of production.

In many other cases, however, cross-border spillovers, arbitrage pressures, and diminished effectiveness of national policies can produce unwanted consequences. In cases involving what economists call externalities (external economies and diseconomies), national governments may need to cooperate to promote mutual interests. For example, population growth, continued urbanization, and the more intensive exploitation of natural resources generate external diseconomies not only within but across national boundaries. External economies generated when benefits spill across national jurisdictions probably also increase in importance (for instance, the gains from basic research and from control of communicable diseases).

None of these situations is new, but technological change and the reduction of tariffs and quotas heighten their importance. When one nation produces goods (such as scientific research) or "bads" (such as pollution) that significantly affect other nations, individual governments acting sequentially and noncooperatively cannot deal effectively with the resulting issues. In the absence of explicit cooperation and political leadership, too few collective goods and too many collective bads will be supplied.

Challenges to Political Sovereignty

The pressures from cross-border economic integration sometimes even lead individuals or governments to challenge the core assumptions of national political sovereignty. Such challenges are a third source of tensions about deeper integration.

The existing world system of nation-states assumes that a nation's residents are free to follow their own values and to select their own political arrangements without interference from others. Similarly, property rights are allocated by nation. (The so-called global commons, such as outer space and the deep seabed, are the sole exceptions.) A nation is assumed to have the sovereign right to exploit its property in accordance with its own preferences and policies. Political sovereignty is thus analogous to the concept of consumer sovereignty (the presumption that the individual consumer best knows his or her own interests and should exercise them freely).

In times of war, some nations have had sovereignty wrested from them by force. In earlier eras, a handful of individuals or groups have questioned the premises of political sovereignty. With the profound increases in economic integration in recent decades, however, a larger number of individuals and groups—and occasionally even their national governments—have identified circumstances in which, it is claimed, some universal or international set of values should take precedence over the preferences or policies of particular nations.

Some groups seize on human-rights issues, for example, or what they deem to be egregiously inappropriate political arrangements in other nations. An especially prominent case occurred when citizens in many nations labeled the former apartheid policies of South Africa an affront to universal values and emphasized that the South African government was not legitimately representing the interests of a majority of South Africa's residents. Such views caused many national governments to apply economic sanctions against South Africa. Examples of value conflicts are not restricted to human rights, however. Groups focusing on environmental issues characterize tropical rain forests as the lungs of the world and the genetic repository for numerous species of plants and animals that are the heritage of all mankind. Such views lead Europeans, North Americans, or Japanese to challenge the timber-cutting policies of Brazilians and Indonesians. A recent controversy over tuna fishing with long drift nets that kill porpoises is yet another example. Environmentalists in the United States whose sensibilities were offended by the drowning of porpoises required U.S. boats at some additional expense to amend their fishing practices. The U.S. fishermen, complaining about imported tuna caught with less regard for porpoises, persuaded the U.S. government to ban such tuna imports (both direct imports from the countries in which the tuna is caught and indirect imports shipped via third countries). Mexico and Venezuela were the main countries affected by this ban; a GATT dispute panel sided with Mexico against the United States in the controversy, which further upset the U.S. environmental community.

A common feature of all such examples is the existence, real or alleged, of "psychological externalities" or "political failures." Those holding such views reject untrammeled political sovereignty for nation-states in deference to universal or non-national values. They wish to constrain the exercise of individual nations' sovereignties through international negotiations or, if necessary, by even stronger intervention.

The Management of International Convergence

In areas in which arbitrage pressures and cross-border spillovers are weak and psychological or political externalities are largely absent, national governments may encounter few problems with deeper integration. Diversity across nations may persist quite easily. But at the other extreme, arbitrage and spillovers in some areas may be so strong that they threaten to erode national diversity completely. Or psychological and political sensitivities may be asserted too powerfully to be ignored. Governments will then be confronted with serious tensions, and national policies and behaviors may eventually converge to common, worldwide patterns (for example, subject to internationally agreed norms or minimum standards). Eventual convergence across nations, if it occurs, could happen in a harmful way (national policies and practices being driven to a least common denominator with externalities ignored, in effect a "race to the bottom") or it could occur with mutually beneficial results ("survival of the fittest and the best").

Each study in this series addresses basic questions about the management of international convergence: if, when, and how national governments should intervene to try to influence the consequences of arbitrage pressures, cross-border spillovers, diminished autonomy, and the assertion of psychological or political externalities. A wide variety of responses is conceivable. We identify six, which should be regarded not as distinct categories but as ranges along a continuum.

National autonomy defines a situation at one end of the continuum in which national governments make decentralized decisions with little or no consultation and no explicit cooperation. This response represents political sovereignty at its strongest, undiluted by any international management of convergence.

Mutual recognition, like national autonomy, presumes decentralized decisions by national governments and relies on market competition to guide the process of international convergence. Mutual recognition, however, entails exchanges of information and consultations among governments to constrain the formation of national regulations and policies. As understood in discussions of economic integration within the European Community, moreover, mutual recognition entails an explicit acceptance by each member nation of the regulations, standards, and certification procedures of other members. For example, mutual recognition allows wine or liquor produced in any European Union country to be sold in all twelve member countries even if production standards in member countries differ. Doctors licensed in France are permitted to practice in Germany, and vice versa, even if licensing procedures in the two countries differ.

Governments may agree on rules that restrict their freedom to set policy or that promote gradual convergence in the structure of policy. As international consultations and monitoring of compliance with such rules become more important, this situation can be described as *monitored decentralization*. The Group of Seven finance ministers meetings, supplemented by the IMF's surveillance over exchange rate and macroeconomic policies, illustrate this approach to management.

Coordination goes further than mutual recognition and monitored decentralization in acknowledging convergence pressures. It is also more ambitious in promoting intergovernmental cooperation to deal with them. Coordination involves jointly designed mutual adjustments of national policies. In clear-cut cases of coordination, bargaining occurs and governments agree to behave differently from the ways they would have behaved without the agreement. Examples include the World Health Organization's procedures for controlling communicable diseases and the 1987 Montreal Protocol (to a 1985 framework convention) for the protection of stratospheric ozone by reducing emissions of chlorofluorocarbons.

Explicit harmonization, which requires still higher levels of intergovernmental cooperation, may require agreement on regional standards or world standards. Explicit harmonization typically entails still greater departures from decentralization in decisionmaking and still further strengthening of international institutions. The 1988 agreement among major central banks to set minimum standards for the required capital positions of commercial banks (reached through the Committee on Banking Regulations and Supervisory Practices at the Bank for International Settlements) is an example of partially harmonized regulations.

At the opposite end of the spectrum from national autonomy lies *federalist mutual governance*, which implies continuous bargaining and joint, centralized decisionmaking. To make federalist mutual governance work would require greatly strengthened supranational institutions. This end of the management spectrum, now relevant only as an analytical benchmark, is a possible outcome that can be imagined for the middle or late decades of the twenty-first century, possibly even sooner for regional groupings like the European Union.

Overview of the Brookings Project

Despite their growing importance, the issues of deeper economic integration and its competition with national political sovereignty were largely neglected in the 1980s. In 1992 the Brookings Institution initiated its project on Integrating National Economies to direct attention to these important questions.

In studying this topic, Brookings sought and received the co-operation of some of the world's leading economists, political scientists, foreign-policy specialists, and government officials, representing all regions of the world. Although some functional areas require a special focus on European, Japanese, and North American perspectives, at all junctures the goal was to include, in addition, the perspectives of developing nations and the formerly centrally planned economies.

The first phase of the project commissioned the twenty-one scholarly studies listed at the beginning of the book. One or two lead discussants, typically residents of parts of the world other than the area where the author resides, were asked to comment on each study.

Authors enjoyed substantial freedom to design their individual studies, taking due account of the overall themes and goals of the project. The guidelines for the studies requested that at least some of the analysis be carried out with a non-normative perspective. In effect, authors were asked to develop a "baseline" of what might happen in the absence of changed policies or further international cooperation. For their normative analyses, authors were asked to start with an agnostic posture that did not prejudge the net benefits or costs resulting from integration. The project organizers themselves had no presumption about whether national diversity is better or worse than international convergence or about what the individual studies should conclude regarding the desirability of increased integration. On the contrary, each author was asked to address the trade-offs in his or her issue area between diversity and convergence and to locate the area, currently and prospectively, on

xxvi   Preface

the spectrum of international management possibilities running between national autonomy through mutual recognition to coordination and explicit harmonization.

HENRY J. AARON   SUSAN M. COLLINS
RALPH C. BRYANT   ROBERT Z. LAWRENCE

Chapter 1

Introduction

THE STOCK markets in most major industrial nations began to fall precipitously in mid-October 1987. Over the next few days, stocks in most national markets lost some 15 to 25 percent of their pre-crisis valuations. Market participants became highly uncertain and concerned about the soundness of financial institutions. To restore confidence, national central banks considered temporary expansions of liquidity in their financial markets. But each central bank's deliberations were troubled by a trade-off dilemma. If an individual central bank chose to act unilaterally, it could probably achieve an easing of domestic financial conditions. Yet it might also trigger a sharp depreciation of the nation's currency. These circumstances led observers, inside and outside of central banks, to propose cooperative adjustments in monetary policies. If the central banks could agree simultaneously to inject temporary liquidity, might not the combined policies have still more favorable effects on market confidence and avert concerns that any one nation's currency would depreciate strongly against the other major currencies?

In 1973–74, and again in 1979–80, the nations in the Organization of Petroleum Exporting Countries (OPEC) sharply raised crude oil prices. These major shocks to the world economy dampened outputs and raised general price levels in industrial nations. The shocks also moved the current account balances of the industrial nations sharply into deficit. Did a danger exist that each oil-importing nation might individually tighten macroeconomic policies to prevent its own current account balance from worsening, with the inadvertent result that macroeconomic policies would be excessively stringent for the world

1

as a whole? Did national governments need to cooperate in choosing their macroeconomic policies?

The preceding examples illustrate circumstances in which national governments could, it is argued, mutually gain from international macroeconomic cooperation. In recent decades, many examples of such circumstances can be identified. Yet protagonists of intergovernmental cooperation have been challenged by numerous skeptics.

For every situation in which an observer has recommended that a major country should act as a potential "locomotive" for the world economy (or, alternatively, that several countries should move together in "convoy"), some other critic has identified potential dangers and argued against the recommendation. The annual economic summit meetings of the largest industrial countries, initiated in 1975, have been variously praised and damned as sites for attempted economic cooperation. For example, the 1978 summit held in Bonn did agree on some jointly designed policies. Followed shortly by the revolution in Iran and the second worldwide increase in oil prices, the 1978 Bonn summit has ever since been an especially controversial example of attempted macroeconomic cooperation. The recessions and protracted high unemployment rates experienced by some nations in the first half of the 1990s stimulated renewed calls for intergovernmental macroeconomic cooperation. Episodes such as these are the testing ground for the ideas and issues examined in this book.

In today's world, nation-states are the primary political units and the dominant locus of governmental decisions. Subnational political jurisdictions such as municipalities are important for local governance. A few international organizations play catalytic roles. But governmental institutions at the level of the nation-state are the most influential political entities, especially for relationships among nations.

Almost all nations have separate currencies, their own central banks, and their own fiscal authorities. Each nation's citizens, and hence the leaders and civil servants of its government, are predominantly concerned with the welfare of own-nation residents. Only residents can vote in national elections. Domestic politics within nations thus have much greater influence than cross-border politics.

Despite the pervasive preoccupation with own-nation welfare, the effects of policies followed in a home nation spill over into foreign nations. Because of these cross-border spillovers, the effective domains of economic markets do not coincide well with governmental jurisdictions. Economic interdependence therefore undermines the policy autonomy of national governments and the controllability of national economies.

Each nation's policymakers are not usually rewarded for any favorable effects caused by their policies abroad. Nor do they tend to be penalized for any bad effects. Policymakers thus typically ignore the foreign effects of their decisions. When cross-border spillovers are ignored in national decisionmaking, however, it is possible for nations collectively to fail in fostering their individual interests. Moreover, cross-border spillovers and the resulting complications have grown larger and more salient over time. In effect, the world has experienced a growing mismatch between its economic and its political structures.

Increasing "arbitrage" incentives, a result of the growing mismatch, tend to erode differences among national policies, regulations, standards, and institutions.[1] If the arbitrage pressures and cross-border spillovers are sufficiently weak, diversity among national economies and polities can persist with only minor challenges. At the other end of the spectrum of possibilities when the pressures and spillovers are strong, national diversity may be so eroded as to force eventual international convergence.

The increasing tensions between national political sovereignty and cross-border economic integration have motivated this entire Integrating National Economies series.[2] In particular, these tensions give rise to the central issues addressed here: when should national governments cooperate in making decisions about their macroeconomic stabilization policies and, if they do so, how ambitious should that cooperation be?

Cooperation could be limited merely to exchanges of information during intergovernmental consultations. But should governments go further, perhaps even attempting to explicitly coordinate their macroeconomic policy decisions? Alternatively, should governments cooperate by agreeing on presumptive guidelines that constrain the use of

1. I use the term "arbitrage" broadly to connote all types of erosion of differences among national economies, not merely in the narrow (more familiar) sense of the erosion of price differentials (buying at one point in geographical space or time and selling at a different price at another).

2. See the preface to this volume.

national policy instruments but still presuppose largely decentralized decisions?

The basic rationale for intergovernmental cooperation is straight-forward. If national decisionmakers take into account the cross-border spillovers of their policy actions, and especially if they consider mutually beneficial adjustments of their policy instruments, each nation may be able to attain higher levels of welfare. Governments may be able, in the jargon of economists, to counteract "externalities" and thereby remedy "market failures" (these terms are defined in chapter 2).

The phrase "may be able" offers a clue to many of the issues discussed in this book. Even though there may be a presumptive case in favor of international cooperation, will any of the various forms of cooperation succeed? Are the potential gains large enough to warrant the effort? Perhaps analytical knowledge about the functioning of national economies and their interactions is too meager to permit cooperation to be feasible? It must also be asked whether efforts to cooperate can turn out to be counterproductive. "Government fail-ures" may exist alongside, or be generated in response to, market failures. One therefore cannot presume that governmental interven-tion to remedy externalities and market failures will invariably prove beneficial.

My treatment of the subject of international macroeconomic coop-eration is selective, sometimes even idiosyncratic. Although I take some background knowledge of economic concepts for granted, I have also tried to summarize technical issues in nontechnical terms. I do not provide a thorough survey of the existing literatures. I have felt relatively free to eschew that task, partly because several useful sur-veys of the economics literature or wide-ranging overviews of the subject have already been published. My book concentrates on the core ideas and on dimensions of the subject that have not been appropriately emphasized in earlier work. The reader will find it easy to dig more deeply into particular aspects of the subject by consulting the references in the footnotes.[3]

3. Surveys or overviews of the subject by economists and volumes that give prominent attention to it, listed roughly in chronological order of preparation, include Hamada (1985); Cooper (1986); Buiter and Marston (1985); Artis and Ostry (1986); Bryant and Portes (1987); Fischer (1988); Horne and Masson (1988); Group of Thirty (1988); McKibbin (1988); Frankel (1988b); Currie, Holtham, and Hughes Hallett (1989); Bran-

My overriding goal is to clarify concepts for the reader and to summarize key analytical points. Chapter 2 thus begins by distinguishing alternative forms of intergovernmental cooperation and introducing the analytical ideas that underpin the entire book. Three analytical perspectives are identified and defined, which in turn are examined in chapters 3, 4, and 5. Chapter 3 uses policy-optimization analysis to examine the basic rationale for cooperation, why such outcomes may occur, and how large the potential gains might be. Chapter 4 focuses on rule analysis of international regime environments. Chapter 5 looks at intergovernmental cooperation through the lenses of institutionalist analysis, a perspective originating mainly outside economics.

Chapters 3–5 shine a relatively beneficent light on international cooperation; for the most part they presume that cooperation is a good thing. Chapter 6 adopts the opposite presumption, focusing on the potential for government failures and the possibility that efforts to cooperate might reduce rather than enhance welfare. Chapter 7 then turns from issues of desirability to questions of feasibility. It emphasizes the ways in which uncertainty about nations' goals and about the functioning of the world economy impedes international macroeconomic cooperation.

To complement the analytical emphases of earlier chapters, chapter 8 discusses the main features and transmission channels of cross-border spillovers among national economies. Chapter 9 reviews key aspects of postwar historical experience, develops some generalizations about that experience, and offers some normative recommendations for the medium-run and longer-run evolution of international macroeconomic cooperation. Chapter 10 briefly recapitulates the main themes of the book and highlights its principal conclusions.

---

son and others (1990), especially the paper by Frenkel, Goldstein, and Masson (1990); Kenen (1990); Canzoneri and Henderson (1991); Dobson (1991); Solomon (1991); Blommestein (1991); Goldstein (1992); and Ghosh and Masson (1994). My views at earlier dates may be found in Bryant (1980, chap. 25; 1987a, chap. 9; 1987b; 1990b). This book is a major revision and expansion of Bryant (1995), an essay in the Princeton University Press volume commemorating the fiftieth anniversary of the Princeton Essays in International Finance.

Chapter 2

Alternative Forms of Cooperation

IN CHAPTER 1, I deliberately used "cooperation," and only that word, to refer to interactions among national governments. But many words beginning with "C" pervade discussion of intergovernmental relations. Much of the analysis in this book, as its title indicates, concerns "coordination." When an amicable nuance for intergovernmental relations is intended, not only cooperation and coordination but terms such as consultation, collaboration, collusion, and coalition are available. C-words with antagonistic nuances include competition, contention, confrontation, conflict, and collision. Unfortunately for clarity, different authors use these words differently, which often leads to confusion (yet another C-word characteristic of intergovernmental relations).

"Cooperation" is best used as an umbrella term for the entire spectrum of interactions among national governments designed to deal with the arbitrage pressures and cross-border spillovers among national economies. "Consultation," "mutual recognition," various forms of "coordination," and "explicit harmonization" are varieties of intergovernmental cooperation, each involving some element of management of the interactions among nations.[1] Consultation alone involves only a small degree of cooperative management. Mutual recognition and coordination are more ambitious, and explicit harmonization still more so. At the opposite extreme of the spectrum, which entails no cooperation and may be labeled "national auton-

---

1. The preface to each of the books in this Integrating National Economies (INE) series uses these distinctions. See Bryant (1987b) for an initial development.

6

omy," the decisions of governments are completely decentralized and no attempt is made to manage the arbitrage pressures and cross-border spillovers.

Top-Level Cooperation: International Regime Environments

International cooperation can be construed as a two-level process. During brief, exceptional episodes of negotiations at a "top level," typically characterized by intensive consultations and bargaining, national governments reach informal understandings or formal agreements defining the processes and institutions through which they will interact with one another. At the time they are reached, such intermittent agreements usually seem to the participating governments to be one-time decisions (though valid for the foreseeable future). Then during the lengthy periods between these top-level negotiations, governments interact through the agreed processes and institutions at a "lower level." At this lower level, each government makes ongoing decisions in a largely decentralized way, independently choosing settings for the policy instruments under its control. The "regime environments" agreed to episodically at the top level can be interpreted as traffic regulations (sometimes loosely called rules of the game) that govern continuing interactions at the lower level.[2]

The regime environments negotiated at the top level are usually labeled simply as "regimes" in the literature on international relations. This use of regime in international relations differs from a second connotation of regime, used widely by economists in analyzing macroeconomic policies within a single nation. Regime in that second sense, to be discussed below, refers to the week-to-week operating procedures used by an individual national central bank (fiscal authority) to implement its monetary policy (fiscal policy). The

---

2. The last century and a half of intergovernmental economic relations has conformed moderately well to this characterization. Economic theorists, notably Hamada (1974, 1977), have applied the idea of two levels of cooperation in game-theoretic analyses of interdependence in macroeconomic policies. I used the distinction in Bryant (1987a). The two-level characterization is implicit if not explicit in much of the literature on international relations among nation-states. For example, Young (1989a, 1989b, 1991) refers to the top-level negotiations as "institutional bargaining" for international society and perceives the national governments as trying to create "constitutional contracts" or "interlocking sets of rights and rules" that are expected to condition their subsequent interactions.

dual connotations of regime can be confusing, especially if—as in this book—both of the two connotations are required in the same sentence or paragraph. When confusion might arise about which meaning is intended, I use "international regime environment" or "international regime" for the first connotation and "national operating regime" or "domestic policy regime" for the second.

My notion of an international regime environment is associated exclusively with episodic, top-level decisions by national governments. The most widely used definition of a regime in the literature on international relations, which captures well the main elements in my notion, is as follows: "sets of implicit or explicit principles, norms, rules and decision-making procedures around which actors' expectations converge in a given area of international relations. Principles are beliefs of fact, causation, and rectitude. Norms are standards of behavior defined in terms of rights and obligations. Rules are specific prescriptions or proscriptions for action. Decision-making procedures are prevailing practices for making and implementing collective choice."[3] Some parts of the international relations literature define regime even more broadly, equating it comprehensively with any patterned regularity in the behavior of national governments interacting with one another. Other international relations authors prefer a more restricted definition, reserving the concept for explicit multilateral agreements among nation-states that regulate national actions within an issue area (in effect, only the rules, but not the principles and norms, in the preceding quotation).[4]

At least two dimensions are involved in identifying an international regime, as suggested in figure 2-1. The horizontal spectrum in figure 2-1 refers to the incidence of agreements and treaties among

---

3. Krasner (1983b, p. 12). See also Keohane (1984, pp. 57–61).

4. Haggard and Simmons (1987) discuss differences among definitions of "regime" in international relations. The concept seems to have been introduced in Ruggie (1975). Keohane and Nye (1977), Keohane (1980), and E. Haas (1980) used it. Two issues of *International Organization* were devoted to the subject in 1982, with much of the material republished in Krasner (1983a); see especially Krasner (1983b, 1983c); Ruggie (1983); Keohane (1983); E. Haas (1983); A. Stein (1983); and Strange (1983). For subsequent discussion, see Keohane (1984); Haggard and Simmons (1987); Young (1986, 1989a, 1989b, 1991); and a special 1992 issue of *International Organization* devoted to multilateralism, which includes contributions by Ruggie (1992); Caporaso (1992); and Kahler (1992). Kahler's book (1995) for this Integrating National Economies series contains further references to the literature on international regimes and institutions.

Figure 2-1. *Alternative International Regime Environments: Characteristics of Interactions among National Governments and International Institutions*

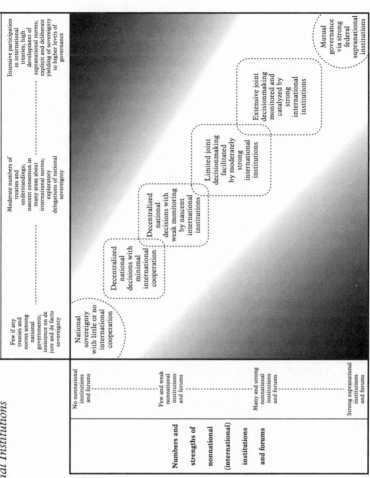

national governments and the principles, norms, rules, and decisionmaking procedures around which actors' expectations converge. The vertical dimension shows the numbers and strengths of nonnational institutions and the forums, processes, and decisionmaking procedures that may be associated with them. Such institutions are "international" or "supranational" in strict senses of those words.[5]

A vertical movement in figure 2-1 from top to bottom involves a shift from complete decentralization of authority among nation-states (northern border) to international regimes in which there is more—but not complete (even at the southern border)—centralization of authority through international or supranational institutions. A horizontal movement from left to right, for any given degree of decentralization, entails more cooperative activity through the establishment of agreed principles and norms and the acknowledgment of constraints (rules and decisionmaking procedures) that have prescriptive and proscriptive force for the "local" decisions of national governments.

The space in the extreme northwest corner of the diagram, a polar case, might be labeled national sovereignty with an absence of international cooperation. For such an international regime, the exclusive determinant of relations among national governments (which would be noncooperative and probably limited) would be the relative powers of the nation-states.[6] As one moves toward the southeast, the regimes still involve essentially decentralized national decisions, but they begin to have elements of international cooperation. With further, larger movements to the southeast, transnational norms and nonnational institutions become more salient, and some aspects of decisionmaking begin to have more centralized dimensions.

International regimes near the extreme southeast corner of the diagram are hypothetical, certainly in today's world and perhaps even throughout the next century. But such regimes can be imagined and can be used as benchmarks for analyzing other spaces in the diagram.[7]

5. For studying some aspects of international cooperation, one would need to make finer distinctions—in particular, for the vertical dimension a distinction between institutions with a regional domain versus those with a global (worldwide) domain. See Kahler (1995).

6. Sovereignty is another concept that often needs clarification and more careful use. My sensitivity to its complex nuances has been raised by a reading of the first chapter of Antholis (1993).

7. The spaces in the southwest and northeast corners of figure 2-1 are presumably irrelevant, even in principle, because of the strong (but not perfect?) positive correlation of the horizontal and vertical sets of variables.

The southeast extreme would entail "mutual governance" facilitated by strong federal, supranational institutions. When dealing with an extensive range of economic and social concerns, national governments might be restricted to "local" roles. Close political union would have evolved, "transnational norms" would presumably be salient, and the locus of political authority would have shifted substantially away from national governments to the federal, supranational level (regionally, globally, or both).

Lower-Level Cooperation: Mutual Recognition and Coordination

Figure 2-2 extends the taxonomy in figure 2-1 to another dimension by considering the interplay between top-level episodic decisions and lower-level intermittent decisions. The vertical axis in figure 2-2 represents the degree of ongoing cooperation affecting lower-level decisions, with little or none at the extreme north and continuous, intensive amounts at the extreme south. The horizontal axis, representing the northwest-southeast diagonal of figure 2-1, arrays the international regimes established in the periodic, top-level negotiations. Several concepts widely used in the literatures on economics and international relations—"autonomy," "mutual recognition," and "international coordination"—can be associated with specific regions in figure 2-2.

National autonomy, in the northwest corner, is one polar case. It is useful as a benchmark in analyzing differing degrees of international cooperation in either or both dimensions. Moving in a southeasterly direction, I identify two regions characterized by *mutual recognition,* one with infrequent consultations and the other with more intensive interactions in the context of internationally monitored presumptive guidelines about which national policies are systemically appropriate. Regions still further to the southeast, with still more ongoing lower-level cooperation and still more structure in the regime environment, are identified as variants of *coordination.* To suggest the spectrum of possibilities, I distinguish three categories of coordination: internationally agreed presumptive guidelines, weak activist, and strong activist. The polar case in the southeast corner may be labeled *federalist mutual governance* with continuous bargaining and joint decisionmaking.

Figure 2-2. *Interplay between Top-Level Intermittent Decisions and Lower-Level Ongoing Cooperation*

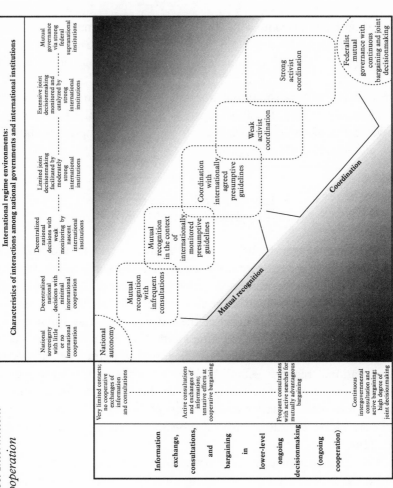

Mutual recognition, a term widely used in discussions about European integration but also applicable in a worldwide context, can be defined narrowly or broadly. Defined narrowly, mutual recognition pertains to regulatory policies, product standards, and certification procedures. Each member state of the European Union (EU), for example, agrees to permit doctors licensed in other EU countries to practice in its country, even if licensing procedures differ in the other countries. Wine or liquor produced in any EU country can be sold in all member countries despite differing production standards. And so on.[8] A broader interpretation of mutual recognition, which I use here, assumes that national governments make decentralized, independent decisions about the whole range of their policies yet to a limited degree acknowledge the interdependence of the separate national policies. Mutual recognition entails minimal traffic regulations and relies on competition among national policies and regulations—through private decisions and market forces—to guide transactions among nations. But mutual recognition also involves exchanges of information and consultations among governments and even nascent reliance on nonnational forums or institutions.

For international regimes embodying more intergovernmental agreements and some international monitoring of the agreements, and especially as intergovernmental consultations become more frequent and intensive, the term mutual recognition becomes less appropriate. Governments may operate under internationally agreed and monitored "presumptive guidelines" that constrain their ongoing policy decisions. In such a situation, the emphasis is not only on (mutually recognized) competition among the decentralized national decisions but also on some agreed norms and constraints that condition the national decisions. As the international monitoring of compliance with such guidelines becomes more important, one might begin to speak of this situation as monitored decentralization. An intergovernmental agreement about exchange rate arrangements, including some guidelines constraining official intervention in exchange markets, would be an example.

8. The term, narrowly interpreted, originates from the 1979 decision of the European Court of Justice in the now famous *Cassis de Dijon* case. Mutual recognition in the narrower European sense is discussed in Wallace (1994) and in several of the chapters in the volume edited by Sbragia (1992a), including those by Guy Peters and Martin Shapiro.

Regions in figure 2-2 still further to the south and east begin to warrant the label "international coordination." The coordination can vary from weak and hesitant to strong and activist. The nature of the coordination depends especially on the frequency and intensity of the ongoing consultations and bargaining, but also on the degree of cooperation built into the international regime as a result of the intermittent top-level decisions.

Because the horizontal and vertical dimensions in figures 2-1 and 2-2 are continuums, no precise boundary exists between the domains of mutual recognition and coordination. Indeed, some analysts might prefer to describe the concepts as partly overlapping. In the diagram presented here, I characterize the northwesterly parts of the coordination region as coordination based on presumptive guidelines. In an earlier version of the diagram, cooperation through internationally monitored presumptive guidelines was located only in the domain of mutual recognition.[9] Nothing of substance turns on whether presumptive-guideline regimes are labeled as mutual recognition, as a weaker form of coordination, or as a combination of the two.

The larger part of the domain of coordination lies to the east, and especially to the south, of mutual recognition. Some significant information exchange and consultation must occur even when the mode of intergovernmental interaction is merely mutual recognition. Still more frequent and intensive consultations will typically occur, however, if the cooperation is sufficiently ambitious to achieve coordination.

What are the essential features of international coordination? To a greater degree than mutual recognition, coordination focuses on cross-border spillovers and the arbitrage pressures eroding the differences among national economies and policies. And coordination is more ambitious in promoting intergovernmental cooperation to deal with these spillovers and pressures. Coordination involves jointly designed, mutual adjustments of national policies—commitments about the time paths of policy instruments, not merely aspirations about the time paths for ultimate-target variables. In clear-cut cases of coordination, bargaining occurs, and governments commit themselves to behave differently—to implement different rules or discretionary settings for policy instruments—than they would have behaved without the coordinating agreement.

9. Bryant (1995, pp. 397, 403).

Strong activist coordination differs from weak activist coordination mainly in the frequency and strength of consultations and bargaining. Strong activist coordination is characterized by fairly continuous rather than intermittent exchanges of information and consultations and by more frequent and intense bargaining about alternative outcomes.

States of the world near the southeast corner of figure 2-2 are extremely hypothetical, but imaginable. International cooperation would have had to intensify to a still greater degree as the economic and political integration of the world became highly advanced. Conceivably, nations could decide to create political institutions that would, for a wide range of concerns, reach centralized decisions for the entire integrated domain. In the extreme, for example, monetary policies for the entire integrated area might be harmonized, with a supranational central bank and, eventually, a single unified currency. The supranational institutions might have a central fiscal budget, which could become an increasingly important part of total governmental expenditures and revenues for the entire integrated area (supranational + national + within-nation local).[10]

If the world polity and economy were ever to go as far as the southeast corner of figure 2-2, the distinction between top-level and lower-level decisions made by national governments could become outmoded. In effect, in such extreme circumstances top-level decisions would be those made by federal supranational institutions, while lower-level decisions would be those decisions that were still made by national governments (now "local" political authorities in the highly integrated area). The situation would have evolved well beyond domains of coordination into federalist mutual governance with continuous bargaining and joint, centralized decisionmaking.[11]

---

10. Important differences between monetary and budgetary policies—not least their macroeconomic stabilization aspects—would arise in such a highly integrated world. "Explicit harmonization" has a relatively clear-cut meaning for monetary policy, but much less so for the different layers of governmental revenues and expenditures. Fiscal policies (still plural, not singular) for such a world would require analysis of all the political and economic issues that have been discussed within federal nation-states under the heading of "fiscal federalism" (see the further discussion below).

11. Figure 2-2 adds some nuances to earlier classifications of cooperation and coordination, for example those of Horne and Masson (1988, pp. 259–63) and Dobson (1991, pp. 2–3). But my taxonomy is broadly consistent with a majority of the earlier discussions.

In the preceding overview, for brevity I speak of "world" political and economic integration, and the harmonization of national policies into world policies. At least for the early decades of the next century, such ideas are likely to have relevance, if at all, for multicountry *regions*—for example, the European Union—rather than for the world as a whole.[12]

The distinctions made in figures 2-1 and 2-2 locate the subject of policy coordination in a larger context. The figures also help to clarify other matters. For example, debates about policy coordination (and, by extension, different varieties of mutual recognition) have paid much more attention to the vertical dimension in figure 2-2 than the horizontal dimension. Protagonists of all positions have implicitly taken as given the international regime they believe to be in place in the world economic system. In effect, they take for granted some point on the horizontal dimension in figure 2-2. Then they focus on the pros and cons of varying the degree and nature of cooperation along the vertical dimension. Most of the economics literature cited in the chapters that follow, for example, is preoccupied with the conduct of lower-level, ongoing decisions. I too believe that many controversial aspects of policy coordination turn on the most appropriate way to conduct lower-level decisions. But some salient aspects of intergovernmental cooperation cannot be thoughtfully appraised when one restricts attention solely to lower-level, ongoing decisions.

Rules and Discretion in National Macroeconomic Policies

I have so far not differentiated among types of government policies. What has been said is relevant for the entire range of governments' policies, microeconomic and regulatory as well as macroeconomic. In the rest of this book, however, I concentrate on policy instruments for which macroeconomic stabilization is the primary objective—that is, on the monetary policies of central banks and the fiscal (expenditure, tax, transfer, and debt) policies of governments.

To discuss macroeconomic stabilization policies in their domestic or international manifestations, one needs to add another dimension to the preceding taxonomy. Accordingly, in this section I discuss the

---

12. Lawrence (forthcoming) examines the tensions between regional and multilateral approaches to economic integration, emphasizing issues of trade policy.

possibilities for national macroeconomic policies running from simple, rigid rules at one extreme of the spectrum to highly activist discretion at the other.

A single nation's monetary or fiscal policymakers try to attain ultimate objectives, which can be stated in terms of desired time paths for the future values of *ultimate-target variables*. The policymakers have at their disposal *instruments* of policy. These instruments are variables that the policymakers can, and do, control precisely at each point in time. The problem of *instrument choice* is to select particular variables as operating instruments. The problem of *instrument variation* is to choose how to vary the settings of the actual policy instruments over time. The way that policymakers resolve the issues of instrument choice and intertemporal instrument variation results in an *operating regime* for policy.

Alternative selections of instruments and alternative procedures for varying them over time give rise to different operating regimes. This definition of an operating regime (national, in effect "domestic") pertains solely to a single nation's lower-level, ongoing decisions for its monetary or its fiscal policies. "Regime" in this sense must be differentiated from the concept of an "international regime environment," defined earlier, and in particular from an international regime embodying intergovernmentally agreed constraints on national policies taking the form of "presumptive guidelines."[13]

Controversy about the conduct of macroeconomic stabilization policies arises from several sources. Differences in views exist about instrument choice, and still more about the relative merits of single-stage versus intermediate-target strategies.[14] Most prominently, however, judgments differ about the role that activism should play in varying the instruments of policy intertemporally (especially for monetary policy). Controversy about the appropriate degree of activism is often couched in terms of the relative merits of "rules" versus "discretion." Activist approaches to instrument variation tend to be de-

13. For elaboration of the (domestic) definition of regime in the economics literature on macroeconomic policy and the identification of alternative regimes for ongoing decisions about national monetary policies, see chapter 1 in the volume entitled *Evaluating Policy Regimes* edited by Bryant, Hooper, and Mann (1993).

14. Intermediate-target and single-stage strategies are defined and discussed in, for example, Kareken and others (1973); Waud (1973); Benjamin Friedman (1975, 1990, 1993); Bryant (1980, chap. 15; 1983, chap. 8); and McCallum (1985, 1990).

fended in the policy community but are often criticized in academic circles. Advocates of activist discretion stress the probable need for policymakers to adjust their instrument decisions in the light of new information about the evolution of the economy or changed perceptions of how the economy does or should function. Critics of activist discretion emphasize the probable benefits of "commitment" of policy to an announced rule; they may also question the availability of reliable information about the evolution of the economy and hence the ability of policymakers to make constructive adjustments in their instrument settings. *Discretion* gives policymakers flexibility in their future actions. *Commitment* to a rule is like a binding contract that specifies in advance the actions that policymakers will (and will not) take.

"Rule" has two connotations frequently encountered in macroeconomics. Sometimes, as in the preceding paragraph, rule is used as an antonym for activist discretion. In that usage, a rule for policy is a determinate procedure, often simple and rigid, indicating how policy will be implemented. Such a rule gives little or no scope to policymakers for activist discretion. At other times, rule has a looser, more general connotation. It may indicate only a prescribed guide for conduct, which need not be simple and rigid and does not necessarily deny policymakers substantial discretion in the future.

In what follows, I reserve the word rule for situations in which the nondiscretionary connotation is dominant. I identify a (domestic) operating regime as a nondiscretionary rule if the regime permits only limited flexibility for policymakers to adjust the settings of their instruments in response to new data, to changes in their perceptions of how the economy works, or to alterations in the numbers or relative importance of their ultimate objectives. Analogously, the more flexibility of these types available to policymakers, the greater the discretion—potential activism—permitted by a particular regime.[15]

15. Any systematic procedure for making decisions can in principle be described by its originators in a manner that permits its replication and implementation by others. With an elastic stretching of conventional language, any systematic procedure, no matter how complex, could thus in some broad sense be construed as a set of decision "rules." (This observation will come up again when I discuss the technical evaluation of alternative types of rule.) Conversely, any systematic procedure for making decisions must be initially selected from a menu of alternative procedures. If the original selection should be judged not to be working well, it may be abandoned. Thus any systematic procedure, no matter how simple or rigid, presumes some degree of "discretionary" choice. To label every systematic method of conducting monetary policy a "rule," or alternatively to describe every operating regime as "discretionary," however, is more likely to foster confusion than insight. Hence the definition suggested for use in everyday discourse presented in the text.

The distinction between operating regimes based on a rule and those characterized by substantial discretion can be elucidated with examples from monetary policy. Suppose the central bank is required to follow an operating procedure whose sole objective is to keep the money stock growing smoothly, day by day, at a fixed rate of growth k, with the value of k not to be changed over time. In real life, the central bank cannot control the money stock exactly from one short-run period to the next. But to implement money targeting, the central bank might use an operating regime (also often referred to as a "reaction function") that can be analytically represented as

(1) $$X_t = X_t^* + \beta[M_t - M_t^*].$$

Here the central bank's operating instrument is a short-term interest rate X_t, X_t^* is the t-period value of the baseline (benchmark) path for the instrument, M_t^* is the target path for the money stock (growing smoothly at the rate k), M_t is the actual value of the money stock, and β is a fixed "feedback" or response parameter summarizing the strength of the responsiveness of X to deviations of M from M^*. Even if β has a modest rather than very high value so that M can differ somewhat from M^* in any particular period, M might track the target path for M^* reasonably well over time. Because the central bank looks only at a single target variable and has essentially no flexibility (other than, perhaps, selecting an initial value for β), this operating regime clearly merits labeling as a rule.

Suppose instead that the central bank pays close attention to several different target variables, Z_{1t}, Z_{2t}, and Z_{3t}. As with the money-targeting reaction function, suppose the central bank specifies target paths for each of these variables and associated feedback parameters governing the responses to deviations of actual from target values. The operating regime might then take the form

(2) $$X_t = X_t^* + \beta_1[Z_{1t} - Z_{1t}^*] + \beta_2[Z_{2t} - Z_{2t}^*] + \beta_3[Z_{3t} - Z_{3t}^*].$$

In this reaction function, the sizes of the feedback parameters relative to each other embody presumptions about the relative importance to the policymakers of the different target variables. Though (2) is less simple than (1), it too leaves little room for flexibility and should be labeled a nondiscretionary rule.

Now consider a variant of (2) that treats the feedback parameters as changeable by the central bank over time and that also includes a term, D_t, permitting discretionary departures from the instrument variation otherwise dictated by deviations of the Z variables from their target paths:

$$(3) \quad X_t = X_t^* + \beta_{1t}[Z_{1t} - Z_{1t}^*] + \beta_{2t}[Z_{2t} - Z_{2t}^*] + \beta_{3t}[Z_{3t} - Z_{3t}^*] + D_t.$$

If the central bank is free from time to time to change the relative sizes of the β feedback parameters and if it frequently chooses nonzero values for D_t (in effect, examining other variables or introducing other considerations into the instrument-variation decision), the operating regime has substantial discretionary elements and should not be labeled a (nondiscretionary) rule.[16]

The debate about nonactivist rules versus activist discretion has a long history. But it took on new intensity in the 1970s and 1980s when inflation rates rose dramatically and economic theory began to focus more intensively on expectations, issues of "time consistency" and reputation, and the potential benefits of credible commitment to an announced policy rule. An operating regime announced by policymakers may be described as time consistent if there is no incentive for the policymakers to change the regime even though they are free to do so. If society is afflicted with an inflation bias, it was increasingly argued in the 1970s and 1980s, policymakers acting in the interests of the society should tie their own hands by commitment to a rule that will, if followed, credibly prevent inflation. The rationale is analogous to Ulysses's behavior in putting wax in his crew's ears and having them tie him to the mast as their ship sailed by the Sirens' rocks.[17]

Four classes of reasons can be identified in determining why one might oppose a discretionary, activist approach to the conduct of monetary policy. First, an opponent of discretion may believe that existing knowledge about macroeconomic behavior and about the impacts of policy actions is so meager that discretionary decisions are likely to do more harm than good. This reason for opposing discretion appeals to uncertainty considerations and asserts that the adverse consequences of uncertainty can best be minimized by adhering to a simple policy rule.

Second, an individual may oppose activist discretion because of a belief that government officials in a democratic-pluralist society are

---

16. Many important features of reaction functions, and several difficult issues, are not captured in these simplified illustrations. My purpose is merely to clarify the distinction between "rules" that have little flexibility and reaction functions that have sufficient flexibility to be treated as "discretionary."

17. Bryant (1980, pp. 294–95).

exposed to irresistible political pressures to pursue incorrect policies. In this view, the political system itself tends to generate deficient macroeconomic policies by sacrificing long-run well-being to short-run political expediency. The example commonly given is the alleged proclivity of policymakers to impart an inflationary bias to the economy when discretionary decisions about monetary and fiscal policies can be influenced by incumbent politicians. The remedy for this political malaise, it may be argued, is to substitute statutory rules or rigid self-denying ordinances in place of discretionary decisions.

The third class of reasons for opposing activist discretion appeals to deficiencies not in the workings of the polity at large but rather in the behavior of government officials themselves. Given human frailty and incompetence, according to this view, it is better severely to limit the discretion of policymakers, thereby reducing the likelihood of mistakes and rascality.

Finally, as already suggested by the analogy of Ulysses and the Sirens' rocks, an opponent of activist discretion may believe that discretion leads to dynamically suboptimal policy decisions and undesirable behavior of the private sector. In this view, a commitment to an announced policy rule will encourage appropriate expectations of policy by the private sector and therefore be more conducive to stable and desirable private sector behavior. The basic assertion is that if private sector expectations are endogenous and "rational," a central bank or government that tries to act in a discretionary way each period may not achieve a better outcome for the economy on average but instead may produce a worse outcome than if it had tied its hands by a committed rule. Opportunistic policy action, period by period, leads the private sector to nullify the efforts of the policymakers.[18]

The debate about rules and discretion—with its associated themes of time consistency, reputation, and the benefits of credible commitment to a simple rule — is one of the most controversial issues about the conduct of economic policies by national governments. It is

18. The first three arguments can be found in the early literature on rules and discretion. For the recent literature—which emphasizes game-theoretic interactions between the decisions of the policymaker and the expectations of the other players, and hence time consistency, credibility, and reputation—pertinent references include Kydland and Prescott (1977); Calvo (1978); Barro and Gordon (1983); Rogoff (1985a, 1985b, 1987); Barro (1986); Fischer (1980, 1990a); Canzoneri (1985); Backus and Driffill (1985a, 1985b); Flood and Isard (1989); Canzoneri and Henderson (1991); and Masson (1994, 1995). Barro (1986) and Fischer (1990a) are helpful overviews.

certain to continue throughout the 1990s and into the next century. Furthermore, this debate has important implications—though the connections are infrequently acknowledged—for the conduct and analysis of international cooperation.

Figure 2-3 emphasizes the interplay between the degree of activist discretion in national operating regimes and the characteristics of international cooperation among national governments.[19] All regions in figure 2-3 can, in principle, be relevant (in contrast with figures 2-1 and 2-2). A situation near the northwest corner is the preferred position for those who dislike discretionary instrument variation in national operating regimes and efforts to cooperate internationally. A position in the southwest region comes closest to characterizing the actual world economy for most of the twentieth century. Policymakers within each national government have tended to use activist discretion in their own decisions about intertemporal instrument variation but have resisted most pressures to agree on international regimes and to engage in intensive consultations and bargaining with other national governments.

The far eastern side of the space in figure 2-3 might characterize a highly integrated world economy in some distant future (although see the discussion below of subsidiarity). Locations near the northeast corner could conceivably be observed if advocates of committed rules were to have their case fully accepted by decisionmakers in federalist supranational agencies responsible for world monetary and central fiscal policies. Locations near the southeast corner would signify that advocates of highly activist discretion had prevailed.

The regions in figure 2-3 of greatest relevance to this book are the three identified prominently in heavy dashed lines. A region in the northwest quadrant (but not the corner region itself) is labeled decentralized, simple-rule national operating regimes. To its east, and partly overlapping, is a region characterized by international coordination focused on rule-based national operating regimes. In both these regions national governments use domestic operating regimes based on simple rules or on rule-like procedures with little discretionary flexibility. The differences between the two regions are a matter of

19. The horizontal dimension for international cooperation in figure 2-3 stems from the northwest-southeast diagonal in figure 2-2, and hence includes both the lower-level, ongoing consultations among governments and their episodic agreements about international regime environments.

Figure 2-3. *Interplay between Characteristics of International Cooperation and Degree of Activism in National Operating Regimes*

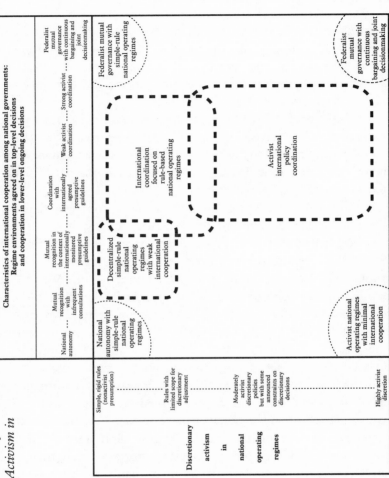

Characteristics of international cooperation among national governments: Regime environments agreed on in top-level decisions and cooperation in lower-level ongoing decisions

	National autonomy	Mutual recognition with infrequent consultations	Mutual recognition in the context of internationally monitored presumptive guidelines	Coordination with internationally agreed presumptive guidelines	Weak activist coordination	Strong activist coordination	Federalist mutual governance with continuous bargaining and joint decisionmaking
Simple, rigid rules (nonactivist presumption)	National autonomy with simple-rule national operating regimes	Decentralized simple-rule national operating regimes with weak international cooperation		International coordination focused on rule-based national operating regimes			Federalist mutual governance with simple-rule national operating regimes
Rules with limited scope for discretionary adjustment							
Moderately activist discretionary policies but with some announced constraints on discretionary decisions							
Highly activist discretion	Activist national operating regimes with minimal international cooperation				Activist international policy coordination		Federalist mutual governance with continuous bargaining and joint decisionmaking

Discretionary activism in national operating regimes

degree; the more important the elements of intergovernmental cooperation (for example, the intensity of international consultations about the rules and the surveillance of compliance), the greater the appropriateness of the label international coordination instead of mutual recognition.

The other prominent region, occupying the central southern space, is the domain of activist international policy coordination. This domain does not extend to the northern border, because activist coordination presumes some discretionary flexibility in the use of national macroeconomic policy instruments.

To make the preceding distinctions more concrete, figure 2-4 identifies certain regions in the space defined by figure 2-3 with historical experience or with prominent proposals for reform of the international regime environment. All of historical experience lies within the western half of the space. Developments since World War II have resulted in some small movements, though all within the southwest quadrant of the diagram. The collapse of Bretton Woods in the early 1970s and the move to much greater flexibility in exchange rates, combined with the failure by the Committee of Twenty to agree on a far-reaching set of proposals for an amended system of more frequently adjusted exchange rates with asset-settlement financing of imbalances, resulted in a modest movement to the southwest.[20] International cooperation was somewhat diminished, and the flexibility of exchange rates encouraged marginally more activism in national operating regimes for monetary policies. Efforts to strengthen multilateral surveillance and cooperation, primarily through Group of Seven (G-7) consultations and economic summit meetings, can be interpreted as a small movement eastward after the mid-1980s.

Figure 2-4 also suggests the rough locations of several reform proposals, all of which would marginally enhance international cooperation. Ronald McKinnon's ideas for encouraging monetary stabilization among the largest industrial countries, sometimes referred to as global money targeting or a gold standard without gold, must be

20. The Committee of Twenty, organized under the auspices of the International Monetary Fund and named after the twenty constituencies constituting the IMF's executive board in the mid-1970s, was charged with negotiating a comprehensive reform of international monetary arrangements. After several years of meetings, agreement could be obtained only for a modest revision of the IMF Articles of Agreement that for the most part endorsed the status quo.

Figure 2-4. *Historical Experience and Proposed Reforms of the International Regime Environment*

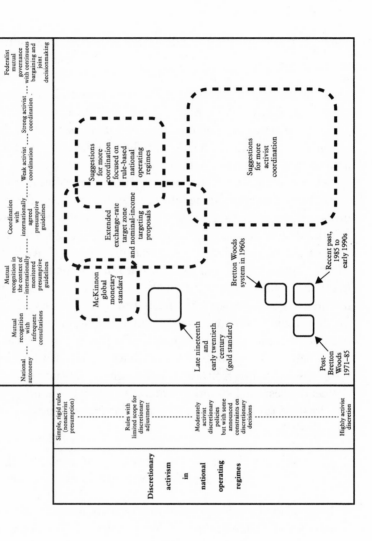

Characteristics of international cooperation among national governments: Regime environments agreed on in top-level decisions and cooperation in lower-level ongoing decisions

placed fairly far north in the diagram, given his suggestions for rules constraining national monetary policies.[21] Target-zone proposals, such as the John Williamson–Marcus Miller "blueprint for coordination," lie to the southeast of McKinnon's proposals but clearly to the northeast of where matters stand today. Williamson and Miller suggest several types of constraints on national operating regimes, with rule-like features but with substantial residual scope for discretionary national policy actions.[22] Jeffrey Frankel's suggestion for international agreement on nominal-income targeting rules should probably be located at roughly the same latitude and longitude as the target-zone proposals; Frankel's suggested rules are much different in substance, but the degrees of decentralization, mutual recognition, and discretionary national actions are similar to those of Williamson and Miller.[23] Suggestions for intensive coordination focused on rule-based national operating regimes, which would entail new one-time international negotiations and significant international surveillance, would mean a major move eastward from the extended target-zone and nominal-income targeting proposals. Proposals for ambitious activist coordination of macroeconomic policies would also require a major move eastward, but from the more southerly latitude of recent experience; the resulting situation would lie well to the south of coordination focused on rule-based national operating regimes.

Market Failures, Government Failures, and the Presumption for Subsidiarity

Because of the rules-versus-discretion controversy, the choice of a north-south latitude in figure 2-3 is contentious. No consensus exists that a movement from north to south, or vice versa, would mean a normative improvement.

What about the choice of an east-west longitude? Should a movement from west to east be regarded as normatively favorable, as indicating progress for the world? The appropriate answer is: no, not necessarily! The presumption for subsidiarity, identified in this section, suggests that an optimal structure of the world polity and

21. McKinnon (1984, 1988).
22. Williamson and Miller (1987).
23. Frankel (1990).

economy might never—not even far into the twenty-first or twenty-second century—involve such extreme centralization and supra-national federalism.[24]

The fundamental rationale for government, at any level, is to foster collective action in contexts in which individual decisionmaking would otherwise produce an inferior outcome. Analysts use terms such as "externalities," "market failures," and "public goods" to refine understanding of this rationale and to evaluate types of governmental interventions.

An externality arises when an activity by one agent affects, favorably or unfavorably, the well-being of other agents who are not decisionmaking participants in (who are external to) the activity. Economic inefficiency often results from externalities, because private costs (benefits) differ from social, collective costs (benefits). Polluting smoke from a factory that causes discomfort to neighborhood residents, for example, creates a negative externality (an external diseconomy). A favorable externality (external economy) occurs when a homeowner beautifies the landscaping on his lot, thereby improving the attractiveness of living in the neighborhood for other residents.[25]

Market failures arise when decentralized private decisions do not result in Pareto-optimal allocations of scarce resources. Externalities of some sort are usually involved in market failures. Because of market failures, collective remedial action that "internalizes the externalities" may be desirable. Such remedial action typically involves the supply of public goods (or amelioration of public "bads"). In the absence of a collective catalyst, public goods tend to be provided

24. I discuss this question because of its intrinsic importance and because of a risk of misinterpretation. Readers of earlier versions of my analysis incorrectly inferred that I intended them to perceive a movement from west to east in figure 2-3 (a movement from northwest to southeast in figure 2-2), because it entails greater international cooperation, as an unambiguous improvement in world welfare. That inference is not what I intend, as the text now stresses.

25. More precise definitions of externalities require that the utility or production relationships for, say, agents B and C be affected by variables chosen by agent A when A does not pay attention to the effects on the welfares of B and C. If A were to receive or pay compensation for the activity that gives rise to costs or benefits for B and C, the situation would not qualify as an externality that creates inefficiency and resource misallocation. The technical literature also makes other distinctions, such as that between *pecuniary* versus *technological* externalities. Key references to this literature are identified in the following footnote.

inadequately, if provided at all (public bads tend to be inadequately ameliorated). Public goods have one or both of two distinctive properties: if a public good is provided, all who value it tend to benefit whether or not they contribute to the cost of providing it; and if a public good is provided to any individual, it is or can be provided at little or no additional cost to others.

Externalities may not cause a misallocation of resources if transactions costs are negligible and if property rights are well defined and enforceable. But in many situations property rights are not well defined, and in practice transactions costs are often nonnegligible. Thus there will often be a potential role for governmental action to try to correct market failures by supplying public goods (or increasing the incentives for others to do so).[26]

The existence of a market failure, however, is not a sufficient condition for government intervention to try to correct it. Government intervention can itself be costly or misguided. In a specific issue area or jurisdiction, whether market failures or government failures are the larger problem can only be settled by empirical analysis.

In virtually every political jurisdiction, even in small localities but especially in larger geographical areas, the interests of residents tend to be heterogeneous and partly in conflict. Unambiguously preferred methods of resolving conflict will seldom exist. The greater the heterogeneity, the larger the likely difficulties. Most consequentially, the interests of the individuals who exercise governmental power in the jurisdiction may differ significantly from the interests of the rest of the population. Such differences will depend on the scope that exists for government officials to advance personal goals by abusing public responsibilities.

Effective government requires accountability and transparency. Their absence makes government failures probable. Without accountability of government organizations and hence of the individuals who lead them, the conflicting interests of the jurisdiction's residents are unlikely to be resolved with everyone's interests being taken into

26. For discussion of the general analytical issues raised by externalities, market failures, and public goods, see Meade (1952); Scitovsky (1954); Bator (1958); Coase (1960); Arrow (1963, 1968, 1974); Kahn (1966); Olson (1971); Baumol and Oates (1975); Schelling (1974, 1978); the contributions in Barry and Hardin (1982); and Oakland (1987). The growing importance of externalities and public goods in modern industrial societies is a major theme in Hirsch (1976).

account. Thus public goods are much less likely to be supplied efficiently. Achieving accountability depends on government actions having substantial transparency. A jurisdiction's government cannot possibly be held accountable if the jurisdiction's residents have inadequate information about the government's goals and activities.

It is not possible to specify in advance and in a contractually binding manner exactly what decisions may have to be taken by government officials in all the conceivable circumstances that may arise. Given this uncertainty, it is practical to grant government officials general authority to formulate and implement a wide variety of decisions. Yet the jurisdiction's residents need to retain a residual right—for example, through periodic elections—to deprive the officials of their authority if the officials are no longer thought to be exercising the authority appropriately. (The situation is partly analogous to that in a collectively owned firm, in which the shareholders grant general "rights of control" to managers but retain the possibility of replacing the managers if the rights are exercised inappropriately.)[27]

Should governance be centralized or decentralized? When there are several layers of governmental jurisdictions, how should powers be allocated among them? Strong general arguments can be advanced for centralization. Centralization may be required in the presence of externalities among jurisdictions, for example when actions in one jurisdiction spill over into others, thus favorably or unfavorably affecting the welfare of other populations. Centralization may be appropriate if the supply of public goods is of higher quality or lower cost when provided through a single rather than multiple jurisdictions. A central governmental authority for a large region may be better able to facilitate redistribution within component local jurisdictions, or especially among component jurisdictions, thereby promoting equity for the region as a whole.

But strong general arguments can also be advanced for decentralization. Local governments may be better informed than central authorities about the preferences of local residents or about conditions affecting the local implementation of policies. Even if a central authority had equally good information, centrally decided policies

27. My observations here and below have benefited from the thoughtful discussion of governance issues in Centre for Economic Policy Research (1993).

could be less responsive to local conditions; the central authority might administratively prefer simple, uniform policies across localities or might feel obliged to implement policies of equal treatment for all its component jurisdictions. Decentralization might also better facilitate the expression of local dissatisfaction with governance and therefore be preferable for encouraging accountability. The residents of a local jurisdiction can manifest dissatisfaction by voting against an incumbent government or even by moving into another jurisdiction.

General arguments cannot resolve this question. In principle, the appropriate allocation of powers will depend on the context and the governmental function. For most modern-day nation-states, political authority is and probably ought to be dispersed across several different layers of government. The responsibilities of each layer need to be shaped by a subtle balancing of the advantages and disadvantages of decentralization.[28]

Of all the general arguments in favor of decentralization, perhaps the weightiest are those pertaining to accountability. When political authority is concentrated and centralized, the risks rise sharply that accountability will be diminished. (The effects of centralization on transparency are more ambiguous, but it seems plausible to argue that transparency too could often be diminished because of the centralization of authority.)

Especially because of the risks from lesser accountability, a presumption exists in favor of subsidiarity. This term, which has origins in Catholic theology, has been widely used in Europe in recent years to discuss alternative allocations of powers within the European Union. The European debate has canvased different models of federation (regionally) and different visions of how a federal Europe might eventually be organized. The continental concepts of subsidiarity and confederation have been contrasted with Anglo-Saxon concepts of federalism (for example, as manifested in the United States).[29]

28. Centre for Economic Policy Research (1993, chap. 3); Cooper (1974); Olson (1969); Oates (1972, 1977); McGuire (1974); and Rubinfeld (1987).

29. See, for example, Peters (1992); Sbragia (1992b); and Centre for Economic Policy Research (1993). The CEPR study distinguishes between federation and confederation as follows: "For our purposes, the critical distinction lies in the degree of sovereignty of the members. In a confederation, the central authority cannot impose decisions on any of its members, since each member has veto power. Indeed, in an important sense there *is* no central authority, merely a mechanism for coordinating the decisions of independent members. In a federation, by contrast, central decisions do not need to be unanimous. If an

Subsidiarity is the presumption that decentralized allocations and exercises of political authority are to be preferred in the absence of compelling reasons for centralization. In other words, lower-level, local jurisdictions should make decisions unless convincing reasons exist for assigning them to higher-level, more central authorities, with the burden of proof always resting on the proponents of centralization.

The presumption for subsidiarity when applied to figure 2-3 argues against a facile inference that a movement from west to east should be regarded as progress. More intensive international cooperation may be, but is not invariably, better than less. For many functional issues, the option of mutual recognition of separately decided national policies will be an appealing first-recourse approach to international cooperation in the remaining years of the 1990s. In effect, national governments would choose decentralized decisions and mutual recognition when possible, would coordinate decisions when spillover externalities were large, and would centralize decisions or delegate significant authority to an international institution only when mutual recognition and coordination were shown to be unworkable.

Alternative Analytical Perspectives

This chapter's cartographical survey of international cooperation has sketched a map of the intellectual territory. What analytical perspective is most useful in studying this territory, especially the categories of mutual recognition and coordination as applied to intergovernmental interactions about national stabilization policies? Each of three perspectives has something to contribute.

Rule analysis concentrates on international cooperation through presumptive guidelines about rule-based national operating regimes. Its preoccupation is with issues that arise within the domains of mutual recognition and the weaker forms of coordination. *Policy-optimization analysis* concentrates on activist policy coordi-

---

appropriate majority of members votes in favour of a measure, this becomes binding on all" (pp. 23–24). J. Ørstrøm Møller, the State Secretary for Denmark's Ministry of Foreign Affairs, outlines a vision of the European Union as a decentralized confederation rather than a "United States of Europe"; see Møller (1995). Peterson (1995) analyzes "functional" and "legislative" concepts of federalism for the United States.

nation. The third perspective can be labeled *institutionalist analysis;* it is not so much an alternative to the other two but rather a broad perspective that can subsume them. Institutionalist analysis represents in part a reaction by noneconomists to the preoccupations of policy-optimization analysis and emphasizes what I subsequently call "satisficing stabilization" and "maintenance of the international regime environment."

Policy-optimization analysis is the most familiar and the most developed of the three perspectives. It dominates the existing literature. Policy optimization grows out of the tradition in economics of studying choices of rational agents; it embeds the logic of rational choice in game-theoretic contexts where two or more agents interact with each other. An analogous tradition is labeled "realism" or "neorealism" in international relations theory.[30] The agents in the analysis are national governments, each of which has well-defined, exogenously given preferences (loss functions) biased toward home-nation welfare.[31] As with the loss functions, the interactions among national economies (how policies and shocks originating in one country affect other countries) and the alternative "strategies" available to governments (choice options) are exogenous inputs to the analysis.

Each national government is treated analytically as an individual decisionmaking agent acting strategically to further its own interest (defined by its loss function). National decisions are seen as plays in "noncooperative games" or, alternatively, "cooperative games." Cooperation and actual coordination characterize outcomes in which the national governments adjust their policy actions to take into account the preferences and actions of other governments. Both the

30. For archetypal references for this analytical perspective in international economics, see Hamada (1985); Cooper (1986); and Canzoneri and Henderson (1991). Representative references in international relations include Waltz (1979); see also Strange (1983). Keohane (1984) is representative of a "modified structuralist" or "neorealist" perspective. Krasner (1983b, 1983c) and Nayar (1995) compare this perspective with others in international relations.

31. The underlying assumption is that citizens of a "home" nation give little or no weight in their utility functions to the welfare of the citizens of "foreign" nations. Hence analysts seeking to study international economics and politics simplify by postulating that each nation's government operates with a "national" loss function. That function is assumed to be predominantly, if not exclusively, a function of home-nation variables. If taken literally, the assumption of a national loss function assumes that each national government behaves as if it is a unitary actor with a capacity unambiguously to rank alternative outcomes and to make rational choices among them.

strengths and weaknesses of this analytical perspective rest on its unitary-actor, rational-choice assumptions.

The policy-optimization perspective has generated valuable insights. Until recently, I have been comfortable discussing issues of international cooperation within that perspective. But some critics see shortcomings in the approach. I, too, am now a bit restive. Hence the attention I give in this book to the complementary perspectives of rule analysis and institutionalist analysis.

Unlike the activist coordination that is a main focus of the policy-optimization perspective, rule analysis presupposes uncoordinated decisions by national governments or decisions that are, at most, weakly coordinated though internationally agreed presumptive guidelines. The national decisions are decentralized, but they are also rule constrained. Rule analysis is based on the presumption that discretionary activism in national decisions about monetary and fiscal policies may have undesirable consequences.

In the rule-analysis perspective, the term "rule" effectively performs double duty. "Rules" can refer to aspects of the international regime environment that have been agreed to serve as constraints on national decisions (for example, limiting exchange rate movements or exchange-market intervention). Such rule features of the international regime, if they exist, will have resulted from past top-level international negotiations. To avoid confusion, I have earlier referred to such rule features as (internationally agreed) "guidelines" rather than "rules."

Rules constraining national decisions, however, may be simply domestic, representing the rule aspects of the nation's own independently chosen operating regimes for monetary and fiscal policies. For example, the nation's central bank may follow a simplified rule for money targeting, nominal-income targeting, or inflation targeting. Though the guideline or rule features of the international regime environment will have been agreed in top-level international negotiations, both the international and the domestic aspects of the operating-regime rules will pertain to the conduct of macroeconomic policies in ongoing, lower-level decisions.

Some authors have used the phrase "rule-based coordination" to refer to international cooperation through presumptive guidelines that constrain nations' simple-rule operating regimes. Advocates of such guidelines hope that the behavior of national governments, when constrained by the guidelines, will generate world macroeconomic outcomes more favorable than would otherwise occur. If more favorable outcomes do occur, one might want to say that the guidelines "implicitly" induce behavior similar or preferable to that achievable through activist coordination.[32] For my taste, it is less likely to cause confusion to use "coordination" for situations characterized by activist bargaining and explicitly agreed mutual adjustment of ongoing decisions about policy instruments.[33]

The institutionalist analytical perspective originates mainly outside economics. One of its distinguishing features is a focus on information exchanges, norms that govern behavior, and the processes through which persuasion and learning take place. More than rule analysis, and much more than policy-optimization analysis, institutionalist analysis emphasizes general principles of conduct and the institutional infrastructure in which they are embodied. Another defining characteristic is an emphasis on "diffuse reciprocity." Still another feature of institutionalist analysis is its concern with the management of crisis periods and, more generally, with the episodic aspects of international cooperation. Indeed, institutionalist analysis focuses not merely on lower-level, ongoing decisions but also, perhaps even especially, on the episodic, top-level interactions that determine international regime environments.

32. Activist explicit coordination conducted via policy optimization will generate Pareto-optimal outcomes (by construction, given the assumptions of the analysis as typically conducted). Advocates of policy optimization thus argue that simplified domestic rules combined with international guidelines cannot produce outcomes more favorable than those attainable with activist explicit coordination. Advocates of rules and guidelines counter this argument by emphasizing the benefits of credible commitment to simple, time-consistent rules and (what they believe to be) the dangers of discretionary activism.

33. Kenen (1990) makes a distinction between "bargaining about specific policy packages" and "a once-for-all bargain about policy rules or guidelines" and refers to the latter as "rule-based policy coordination." My terminology and his are somewhat inconsistent, because I emphasize the distinction between policy activism versus simple-rule operating regimes and hence must consider the domestic as well as international features of rule-based policies. But the differences between Kenen and me are only semantic. Note, for example, his description of the Bretton Woods system as "too vague to meet my definition of full-fledged coordination" because, although "the exchange rate obligations were explicit," "the corresponding policy commitments were implicit" (p. 67). The presumption in the IMF Articles of Agreement about national operating regimes was that they would be relatively activist and discretionary, not rule based.

Chapter 3

Coordination Analyzed through the Lenses of Policy Optimization

*I*N THIS CHAPTER, I look through the lenses of the policy-optimization perspective at the more ambitious forms of international cooperation labeled earlier as activist coordination. Many of the resulting insights have by now become familiar in the literatures about international cooperation in open-economy macroeconomics and in international relations.

Basic Rationale for Coordination

Applications of game theory in economics make more precise a commonsense insight that has been recognized in political and economic theory for centuries: decentralized, noncooperative decisionmaking can produce outcomes that are decidedly inferior to a set of efficient, Pareto-optimal outcomes attainable through collective action. Numerous studies of strategic interactions identify instances in which unconstrained maximization by individual decisionmaking agents, while rational for each agent, can produce suboptimal outcomes for all agents together. The basic concepts that analysts use to evaluate these strategic interactions—externalities, market failures, and public goods—have already been identified in chapter 2.

Most analysis of externalities, market failures, and hence the possible suboptimality of decentralized decisions has pertained to interactions among agents within some national economy. But analogous issues arise for many types of interactions among nations and their governments. Increasing economic integration across national borders generates a growing variety and intensity of collective-action problems with international dimensions. In principle, therefore, when transnational externalities are important and if coordination among national governments is feasible, it may be possible to internalize the externalities by reaching mutually preferable outcomes through cooperative decisionmaking. This fundamental insight about international cooperation is the starting point for most of the literature adopting the policy-optimization perspective.[1]

A closely related insight is the appreciation that neither international cooperation nor activist coordination is a synonym for altruism or benevolence. On the contrary, cooperation and coordination can result from completely selfish bargaining. Coordination does not require that national governments have common or even compatible goals, or that some governments must sacrifice their own goals in deference to the goals of others. With some exceptions, goals are not identical among nations. The natural presumption is that each government gives primacy to the welfare of its own citizens. Cooperation and coordination merely imply the self-interested mutual adjustment of behavior. Most important, the potential for large gains from cooperation in all its forms may well be greatest when goals are inconsistent and discord is high.[2]

Activist coordination of macroeconomic stabilization policies should not be confused with "harmonization." The harmonization of national policies and standards (alternatively stated, the evolution of "world" policies and standards) is an extraordinarily advanced form of international cooperation. It can be imagined for the hypothetical regions along the eastern border of figure 2-3 (federalist mutual governance). Examples of such harmonized policies might be product standards, tax policies on income from capital, and regulations for

1. References to the older game-theory and market-failure literatures as applied to international macroeconomic issues are given in Bryant (1980, chap. 25). See Canzoneri and Gray (1985); Canzoneri and Henderson (1991); and Ghosh and Masson (1994) for more recent references. The earliest discussions of the basic insight applied to international cooperation include Niehans (1968); Hamada (1974, 1976, 1979); and Cooper (1968, 1969).

2. This point is not always appreciated, even by economists. For example, Martin Feldstein, writing for the *Wall Street Journal* editorial page, makes the puzzling and incorrect remark that "because foreign governments will inevitably pursue the policies that they believe are in their own best interests, it was inevitable that international coordination would eventually collapse." See "The End of Policy Coordination," November 9, 1987.

supervising financial intermediaries.[3] In the limit, as noted earlier, one can even imagine currency unification and a single world or region monetary policy (which would harmonize monetary policies "completely" across nations).[4] Even under federalist mutual governance, however, not all types of national ("local") governments' policies would be harmonized—most notably, budgetary policies. The presumption for subsidiarity and the principles of fiscal federalism would still justify substantial decentralization for many governmental budgetary decisions.[5]

The differences between coordination and harmonization are fundamental. Normally, one would *not* expect coordinated national monetary and fiscal policies to be harmonized. For example, national governments would not necessarily adjust policies in the same directions, with every government contracting or every government expanding. Heterogeneity might well prevail even for the hypothetical case of all governments undertaking "optimal" coordination. If asymmetric disturbances hit their economies, optimal policies will typically require governments to do different things. For example, one nation might need to ease monetary policy while others tightened. The further the distance away from the eastern border in figure 2-3, the less likely that harmonization would be an appropriate benchmark for "full coordination."

Why May Coordination Occur?

Cooperation, and still more so coordination, pose a theoretical problem for game-theoretic analysis of strategic interactions among individual decisionmakers. The basic results in the theory, often expounded in terms of game situations such as the prisoner's dilemma, explain why noncooperative decisions may be dominant strategies for most or all agents. Free riders, so labeled because they enjoy benefits

3. For discussion of international cooperation, including harmonization, in these areas, see the books in this Integrating National Economies series about product standards by Sykes (1995); taxation by Tanzi (1995); and financial regulation by Herring and Litan (1995).

4. See, for example, the INE book by Eichengreen (1994).

5. On fiscal federalism, see, for example, Oates (1972, 1977, 1985); Olson (1969); McGuire (1974); and Rubinfeld (1987). For tax policies, see Gordon (1983); Wilson (1986); Emerson and others (1988); Sinn (1990); Kanbur and Keen (1993); and Centre for Economic Policy Research (1993).

without contributing to costs, inhibit cooperative decisionmaking. The "supply of cooperation" is likely to fall short of what would be mutually beneficial because collective action is a public good. Interdependent groups of agents, with their individual members making decentralized (rational) decisions, may fail to foster their common interests.[6] These general points seem to apply with even greater force to a situation in which national governments are the individual decisionmaking agents. How is it, then, that intergovernmental cooperation and coordination do sometimes occur?

Policy-optimization analysis has explored three categories of explanation for the emergence of cooperation. First and most straightforward, bargaining to reach a cooperative outcome that is Pareto-efficient may require side payments. In the international context, for example, some national governments that ought to be included in a cooperative agreement may not have sufficient incentives to participate. Only if such free-rider governments can be bribed through side payments of some sort, thereby raising their own gains from cooperation, will they be willing to help other prospective participants move the outcome toward the Pareto-optimal frontier. Allowing for the possibility of side payments—perhaps even encouraging their use—can thus help to overcome the resistance to cooperation.

The second line of reasoning to explain the existence of cooperation is to focus on repetition of the strategic interactions and hence on the phenomena of reputation and credibility. Most of game theory initially explored games that, analytically, were played only once. Especially in such one-shot games, illustrated by the prisoner's dilemma, the strategy of defection (not to cooperate) typically dominates. Once the assumption of a single episode of strategic interaction is relaxed, however, the range of possible outcomes is greatly increased. Analysis must then focus on strategic time paths rather than single moves. Issues of trustworthiness and credibility, and contingent cooperation, can become paramount. Broadly speaking, cooperative outcomes are more often observed in repeated than in one-shot games.[7]

6. For discussion, see, for example, Olson (1971) and Hirsch (1976) and the other references in chap. 2, note 26.

7. For theoretical discussion of repeated games, see, for example, Kreps and others (1982); Kreps and Wilson (1982); Hardin (1982); Axelrod (1984); and Taylor (1987).

Some strategies for such iterated games call for contingent or "conditional" cooperation. A conditional cooperator agrees to cooperate only on the condition that some or all of the other participants in the game will also cooperate. The "tit-for-tat" strategy explored extensively by Robert Axelrod and others is the most prominent example of a conditional strategy.[8] By definition, conditional cooperators have to monitor the actions of other players to enforce compliance with the cooperative decisionmaking. The study of repeated games therefore involves careful analysis of enforceability. So-called trigger strategies, associated with the monitoring of key observable variables that indicate whether participants may be "reneging" on a cooperative agreement, may be used by conditional cooperators to decide whether to continue their cooperative behavior. Matthew Canzoneri and Dale Henderson explore these issues in detail for the case of international cooperation in monetary policies.[9] They show how policymakers in a repeated game, if they do not discount the future too heavily, can make decisions in a decentralized manner without explicit coordination but nonetheless produce outcomes resembling those attainable through explicit coordination.

The third type of explanation for the emergence of cooperation focuses on leadership and the formation of a cooperating subgroup by some of the participants in a game situation. The traditional free-rider analysis, which predicts a suboptimal supply of collective action, tends not to give adequate emphasis to the potential role of leadership. Imaginative political entrepreneurship can sometimes circumvent the inability of unorganized groups to cooperate by packaging the potential benefits in a fashion that induces collective action.[10] Not all of the n agents in a strategic situation, moreover, need necessarily cooperate. It may be possible for a k subset of the n agents to form a smaller group, members of which agree to cooperate regardless of what the remaining $n - k$ agents choose to do.[11]

8. Axelrod (1984).

9. Canzoneri and Henderson (1991, chaps. 4, 5).

10. See, for example, Frohlich, Oppenheimer, and Young (1971); and Young (1991). Olson acknowledges the validity of this point in the appendix to the second edition of *The Logic of Collective Action* (1971, pp. 176–77).

11. Applications of these ideas to intergovernmental cooperation are numerous—see, for example, Canzoneri and Henderson (1991, chap. 3) and Kahler (1992). The theory of "hegemonic stability" emphasizes the leadership of a hegemon in facilitating desirable systemic outcomes; see Kindleberger (1973); Gilpin (1975); and Keohane (1984). For critical evaluations of this theory, see Snidal (1985); and Grunberg (1990).

Despite the possibility that a subgroup may coalesce around a cooperative outcome, the forces that threaten cooperation may still be significant. Indeed, it has been another fundamental insight of the policy-optimization perspective to point out that cooperative solutions tend to be more difficult to attain in larger than in smaller groups. The original statement of this conclusion by Mancur Olson rested on three assertions: that the fraction of a collective benefit enjoyed by any individual agent tends to decline as the size of the group increases; that larger groups are less likely to exhibit the small-group strategic interactions that facilitate the supply of collective goods; and that organization costs tend to increase with an increase in group size.[12] Authors such as Russell Hardin and Michael Taylor take issue with the last two of these assertions; their arguments have been summarized by Miles Kahler.[13]

Taylor emphasizes still another reason for believing that larger groups have more difficulty than smaller groups in achieving collective action. He observes that conditional cooperation becomes more difficult as the size of a cooperating group grows. Cooperation and coordination tend to be sustainable only when conditional coopera-tors play an important role. But conditional cooperators need to monitor the compliance of others, and the costs and difficulties of monitoring compliance tend to increase with the number of partici-pants.[14] International economics and intergovernmental political agreements provide numerous illustrations of this phenomenon.

How Large Are the Potential Gains?

The literature on policy optimization applied internationally has naturally devoted considerable attention to the size of the potential gains from intergovernmental cooperation and, more narrowly, from the activist coordination of macroeconomic policies. How much has been learned about this question, from exploring small theoretical models or from examining empirical models?

The first point to stress is that significant gains may result merely from governments' acting strategically rather than in an insular or

12. See Olson (1971, p. 48).
13. Hardin (1982); Taylor (1987); Kahler (1992).
14. Taylor (1987, p. 105).

myopic manner. Some benefits may be achieved, in other words, by moving from outcomes where international interdependence receives little attention to outcomes where national decisions are decentralized yet governments exchange information about their economies and policies. Information exchanges need not entail governmental attempts to move all the way to explicit activist coordination of national policy instruments.

The literatures on international relations and international economics have long conjectured that "mere" consultations and information exchanges are extremely important aspects of international cooperation.[15] Information exchanges about the "initial conditions" in which economies are currently located and about the shocks they are thought to be currently experiencing can help to reduce uncertainty and thereby facilitate national decisions even when there is no intention of explicitly coordinating policies.

Some limited evidence supports this favorable view of consultations and information exchanges. I know of none that generally contradicts it. Andrew Hughes Hallett, for example, carried out some loss-function calculations showing that the welfare gains for the United States and Europe associated with moving from a baseline situation to a so-called noncooperative solution (that is, to optimized policies with strategic behavior) were larger than the further gains associated with moving from that noncooperative solution to a fully coordinated solution.[16] Matthew Canzoneri and Patrick Minford, and Hali Edison and Ralph Tryon, also report estimates affirming that large gains are attainable when nations act strategically rather than myopically (insularly).[17]

Canzoneri and Edison, in another paper, study gains realizable from information exchanges and surveillance and from agreement about instrument choice. They envisage national policymakers making decentralized decisions to reach a Nash noncooperative solution. Yet the policymakers are really made to choose between alternative Nash noncooperative outcomes; they settle on a "good" equilibrium with properties dominating other Nash solutions. This equilibrium is

15. For examples, see Keohane and Nye (1977); Keohane (1984); Bryant (1987b); and Currie, Holtham, and Hughes Hallett (1989).
16. Hughes Hallett (1986a); and Brandsma and Hughes Hallett (1989).
17. Canzoneri and Minford (1989); and Edison and Tryon (1988).

self-enforcing in the sense that monitoring by a world policeman is not required. Canzoneri and Edison also calculate the gains connected with moving from one of the Nash noncooperative outcomes to an outcome characterized by full-scale cooperation. Their principal conclusion is that the gains from information sharing and from agreement on instrument choice tend to be much larger than the incremental gains from going further to full-scale cooperation (activist coordination).[18]

Estimates of the gains resulting from optimized strategic interaction of the type cited in the preceding paragraphs cannot be regarded as definitive evidence about the potential gains from information exchanges among national governments. Such calculations do not clearly distinguish between (1) gains associated with efficient use of information about cross-border spillovers and foreign governments' loss functions versus (2) gains associated with efficient use of information about a country's own economic structure.

It is possible to imagine circumstances in which certain types of information exchange among governments could lower welfare. Rex Ghosh and Paul Masson construct an example that stems from a simple model of official exchange-market intervention. In their model, governments exchange information that is asymmetrically available about certain types of shocks.[19] What makes the Ghosh-Masson illustration produce its welfare-reducing result is the temptation of one government to mislead another given that the governments are merely sharing information rather than making policy commitments.

I initially perceived this Ghosh-Masson example as contrived and potentially misleading rather than providing insight into the likely welfare consequences of intergovernmental communications and exchanges of information. An institutionalist analyst appraising this illustration might regard it as an example of policy-optimization analysis gone astray (see the discussion in chapter 5). The institutionalist could emphasize the continuous dealings that governments have with one another in the context of existing international regimes. Because of those dealings, he could argue, any clearcut effort to

18. Canzoneri and Edison (1990). The terminology in this Canzoneri-Edison paper is inconsistent with my terminology. "Coordination" for Canzoneri and Edison is the process of agreeing on the preferred Nash noncooperative solution. Their (full-scale) cooperation is my activist coordination.

19. Ghosh and Masson (1994, chap. 7).

deceive in period t is likely to become apparent in period $t + 1$ or $t + 2$. Hence the norms and institutional-process aspects of the international regime would discipline the communication of information and discourage such deception-motivated information exchanges.

After reflecting on comments on the initial draft of this book made by Masson at a review conference, however, I came to believe that it is appropriate to stress, as Ghosh and Masson do, the potential for misleading as well as productive intergovernmental exchanges of information. When governments have conflicting goals and hence potential incentives to misinform one another, they may well act on those incentives if they believe their deception will go undetected and their reputations remain unsullied. (In his comments in this volume, Masson gives some examples.) Although I believe that, in practice, most intergovernmental information exchanges will enhance rather than diminish global welfare, I agree with Masson that attention needs to be paid to instances when that presumption is not correct.

The lion's share of attention in the policy-optimization literature has been given to the size of potential gains attainable from choosing a cooperative solution embodying activist coordination (sometimes referred to as full coordination). Analytically, the issue is typically posed as the size of potential gains associated with moving from a Nash noncooperative solution to a solution characterized by Nash bargaining.[20]

Many studies have tackled this question since the initial paper by Gilles Oudiz and Jeffrey Sachs.[21] Many investigations have been conducted in the context of smaller theoretical models.[22] A variety of others have used one or more empirical models.[23]

20. In models where intertemporal dynamics are explicit, several alternative types of Nash noncooperative solutions can be defined. Nash cooperative bargaining solutions can also vary, of course, with alternative specifications for national and "joint" loss functions. Thus a precise analysis of the question identified in the text is more complex than it may at first appear. Because the activities of consultation and information exchange cannot be rigidly compartmentalized from activist coordination, furthermore, it is also difficult to separate the potential gains associated with "mere" consultation from the potential gains achievable through activist coordination.

21. Oudiz and Sachs (1984).

22. These include Oudiz and Sachs (1985); Carlozzi and Taylor (1985); Currie and Levine (1985); Miller and Salmon (1985); John Taylor (1985); Levine and Currie (1987); Ghosh (1986); Turnovsky and d'Orey (1986); Turnovsky, Basar, and d'Orey (1988); van-der-Ploeg (1988); Ghosh and Ghosh (1991); Masson (1992); and Ghosh and Masson (1994).

23. These contributions include Hughes Hallett (1986a, 1986b, 1987, 1989); Currie,

It has become conventional wisdom, based on the empirical studies, to say that the incremental gains from coordination for the largest economies in the Organization for Economic Cooperation and Development (OECD) are small or at most modest in size. The original Oudiz and Sachs study suggested incremental gains on the order of .5 of 1 percent of real GNP, or less.[24] Most of the other studies fail to show substantially larger gains. As shown by (among others) Gerald Holtham and Andrew Hughes Hallett, Jeffrey Frankel and Katherine Rockett, and Ellen Nedde, however, estimates of the size of the gains are significantly sensitive to the models used and the definitions of the noncooperative and cooperative solutions.[25] In any case, potential gains on the order of .5 of 1 percent of real GNP are far from negligible, even though, as emphasized by David Currie, Holtham, and Hughes Hallett, the forecast standard errors of target variables tend to be this large.[26]

The prudent stance on this question has not changed much since my earlier conclusion.[27] The existing evidence is inconclusive. The sensitivity of the estimated gains to different models and to alternative specifications of the underlying assumptions needs to be studied further. Canzoneri and Henderson review only the theoretical literature, but they too suggest that "the jury is still out" on the size of the potential gains from activist coordination.[28]

The presumption that activist coordination could yield sizable gains is decidedly stronger for coordination among larger than among smaller countries. Many individual nations are relatively "small": actions taken by their policymakers or nonpolicy disturbances originating in their economies tend to have only minor effects on macroeconomic variables in the rest of the world. Sizable systemic externalities are thus much more likely to result from, say, a fiscal

---

Levine, and Vidalis (1987); Canzoneri and Minford (1988, 1989); Edison and Tryon (1988); Frankel and Rockett (1988); Brandsma and Hughes Hallett (1989); Hughes Hallett, Holtham, and Hutson (1989); Holtham and Hughes Hallett (1987, 1992); Ghosh and Ghosh (1991); several of the contributions in Currie and Vines (1988); Nedde (1989); Canzoneri and Edison (1990); and Ghosh and Masson (1988, 1991, 1994).

24. Oudiz and Sachs (1984).

25. Holtham and Hughes Hallett (1987, 1992); Hughes Hallett (1987); Frankel and Rockett (1988); Nedde (1989).

26. Currie, Holtham, and Hughes Hallett (1989, p. 26).

27. Bryant (1987b).

28. Canzoneri and Henderson (1991, p. 135).

action taken by the United States than from a fiscal action taken by Denmark. Other things being equal, the economically largest countries—the United States, Germany, and Japan—should worry the most about the cross-border spillovers stemming from their economies. And those countries should be the most alert to the potential gains from activist coordination.

Nonetheless, small countries should not be exempted from participation in intergovernmental cooperation. *Every* nation has a selfish stake in promoting an improved functioning of the world economy. Indeed, the smallest countries may even reap per capita gains that exceed the per capita gains for large countries. If the many small countries in the world economy each act as a free rider, presuming that international cooperation is the sole province of large countries, the probability of cooperation and coordination will be low. The appropriate principle is straightforward. No country should be regarded as so small that it can justify standing on the sidelines altogether, or ignoring the consequences of its actions—or inactions—for other countries.

Chapter 4

Rule Analysis of International Regime Environments

POLICY-OPTIMIZATION analysis presumes that national governments should be able, through international consultations and bargaining, to make mutually agreed-on, discretionary adjustments of the policy instruments in their national operating regimes. But advocates of rules for national operating regimes are uncomfortable with the activist resetting of national instruments associated with activist international coordination. Not surprisingly, therefore, rule advocates prefer to distance themselves from many aspects of policy optimization.

Main Focus of Rule Analysis

Rule analysis of international cooperation, in contrast to policy optimization, is preoccupied with the evaluation of alternative international regime environments and their associated national operating regimes. As indicated in figure 2-3, rule analysis rests on the premise that ongoing decisions about national macroeconomic policies will not be explicitly, actively coordinated but rather will be constrained by simple-rule or rule-based national operating regimes. It envisages mutual recognition, or perhaps weak forms of coordination, as the typical mode of international cooperation. Each nation's decisions are primarily conditioned by its own rule-based operating regimes. International cooperation can be significant if the initial choice of domestic operating regimes is subject to top-level international consultation and agreement. Subsequent international cooperation, if any, however, is limited to exchanges of information and (perhaps) monitoring by international organizations.

Some advocates of decentralized simple-rule operating regimes, or international coordination focused on rule-based operating regimes, regard such international regimes as unambiguously first best—better than more ambitious forms of cooperation such as activist coordination. Other advocates support such international regimes as an attainable second best. They believe that activist full coordination is not feasible and that coordination focused on rule-based operating regimes may be able to emulate some of the favorable consequences that would be achieved if full coordination were feasible.

Rule analysis must somehow evaluate the likely performance of national economies under alternative international regime environments and rank the international regimes against one another. The analytical task is analogous to that involved in evaluating alternative domestic operating regimes for monetary or fiscal policy in a single economy. Analysts must have at their command one or more structural models of macroeconomic behavior that represent, *endogenously*, not only the key aspects of private behavior but also the main features of the policymakers' behavior. The behavior of the policymakers is represented by reaction functions, which summarize how the actual instruments of monetary and fiscal policy vary intertemporally in response to evolution of the economy.

Reaction-function equations for a structural model are derived, explicitly or implicitly, from policy loss functions (which could be, but do not have to be, well-defined specifications of preferences for a "unitary actor"). Illustrations of a reaction function were shown above in chapter 2 in equations (1) through (3). In general, such functions take the form

$$(4) \qquad X_t \quad = \quad X_t^* \quad + \quad f(G_t - G_t^{U^*}) \quad + \quad D_t$$

actual value of policy instrument	ultimate-target or benchmark value of instrument	responses to disequilibrium deviations of goal variables	nonmodeled residual elements of policy

where X is the particular policy instrument whose behavior is summarized, G represents a vector of the policymakers' ultimate-target variables, and G^{U^*} is a corresponding vector of the desired paths for those variables. As observed earlier, if the nonmodeled residual elements of policy D_t can regularly take on nonzero values, the reaction function has substantial discretionary elements. Most nondiscretionary rules therefore omit D_t altogether or give it only a minor role.[1]

Rule analysis in an international context, however, is even more complex. The structural models that are a prerequisite for the analysis must be *multicountry* models, because the overriding purpose is to evaluate the performance of international regimes, taking into account the cross-border as well as domestic effects of macroeconomic policies and nonpolicy shocks. And separate reaction functions are required to represent the behavior of each nation's monetary and fiscal authorities. In effect, every international regime to be studied must be a complex combination of the domestic operating regimes of each country or region represented in the corresponding structural model.

One fundamental goal of rule analysis is to assess the performance of alternative international regimes in stabilizing ultimate-target variables in the face of various economic disturbances (nonpolicy shocks and policy actions themselves). A related issue, important for the analysis of some types of rules, is to assess the ability of any one nation's policymakers to identify in a timely and accurate manner the disturbances that are hitting the national economy.

The potential benefits from credible commitments to simple, time-consistent rules is still another major subject for analysis. Analysts need to quantify these benefits for different international regimes and to rank the international regimes against one another on this dimension. Alternatively stated, analysts need to understand how credibility is earned for various international regimes (and for their national component regimes) and how it can be eroded by various types of discretionary departures from a particular international regime. Not least important, rule analysis should be able to examine the possibly difficult trade-offs between the commitment properties and the stabilizing properties of international regimes.

Unresolved Analytical Issues

A domestic operating regime is a nondiscretionary rule if the regime permits only limited flexibility for policymakers to adjust the

---

1. The reasons why structural models used for rule analysis must include explicit endogenous equations for the behavior of policymakers and the difficult issues of how to specify reaction-function equations are discussed in Bryant (1991a) and Bryant, Hooper, and Mann (1993).

settings of their instruments in response to new data, to changes in their perceptions of how the economy works, or to alterations in the number or relative importance of their ultimate objectives. Although that definition is appropriate for the level of discourse here, more precision would be called for in technical research evaluating alternative regime environments.

An analytical attempt to summarize the real-life behavior of policymakers must highlight the main influences shaping that behavior. Fine details and subtle nuances will be omitted altogether or at best represented by imperfect approximations. The more discretionary the behavior of policymakers (in the sense of conventional language), the more difficult it becomes to capture the behavior in an analytical approximation.

Moreover, any analytical approximation of the manner in which policymakers define their goals and adjust the settings on their instruments in response to new data will result, in technical discourse, in a representation of the operating regime that makes it appear like a nondiscretionary rule. Even a highly complex strategy for conducting policy, which in everyday discourse would unambiguously be termed a discretionary regime, must be represented as a (complex) "rule" for the purposes of technical discourse. Equation (3) in chapter 2 is an illustration of that point. The substantive differences between discretionary regimes and rule regimes (conventional language) of course remain significant at the level of technical discourse. The rule-like appearance of all analytical representations at a technical level is, from the perspective of the substantive debate about rules versus discretion, a superficial resemblance.

In technical research, how simple does a reaction-function equation have to be before it merits the label of a simple, nondiscretionary rule (everyday discourse)? Is it merely the number of right-hand-side, goal variables in the equation, together with their associated feedback coefficients, that determines whether to consider the policy behavior a simple rule? How limited must the number of goal variables and feedback coefficients be before an analyst can qualify the policy behavior as a simple rule instead of an activist response to the economy's evolution? Should the reaction-function equation contain, if not a D_t term, then at least a residual term (what some might call an error), and if so how should it be treated in the analysis? How should one specify reaction functions for fiscal policy, and the interactions of

fiscal policy with monetary policy, so that the structural model en-
forces each national government's intertemporal budget constraint
(the issue of intertemporal fiscal closure rules)?[2]

I mention these difficult and unresolved research problems because they have potentially great significance for the rule analysis of
international regime environments. These issues have not yet been
addressed carefully in the research on presumptive guidelines for
international economic coordination.

Stabilization Properties of Regimes

The stabilizing properties of alternative international regimes have
received most of the attention in the limited research carried out thus
far. Some of that research has focused on simplified theoretical models for which analytical solutions can be obtained. More complex
structural models require simulation analysis. Most studies working
with multicountry empirical models have used the techniques of
deterministic simulation, examining the consequences of a series of
individual shocks. In a few cases, researchers have employed the
techniques of stochastic simulation, in which the shocks passed
through a structural model are random draws from the model's own
residuals, with the shocks occurring to multiple variables and varying
in size from period to period. In principle, stochastic simulation
provides a more realistic basis for evaluating the robustness of alternative international regimes in stabilizing ultimate-target variables in
the presence of multiple shocks.

The most comprehensive effort thus far undertaken to analyze
alternative national operating regimes in an international setting
stems from a collaborative project of multicountry modeling groups.
The volume resulting from the project contains illustrations of all the
complementary approaches.[3] The strategy of the project was to get

---

2. On the analytical aspects of intertemporal fiscal closure rules for fiscal policy, see
Bryant and Zhang (1995).

3. Bryant, Hooper, and Mann (1993). See the analyses with simplified theoretical
models in chap. 2 by Henderson and McKibbin; deterministic simulations summarized in
chap. 4 and included in individual papers; and stochastic simulations in chap. 5 and
individual papers.

the ten participating model groups to run "horse races" among four highly simplified intermediate-target regimes for national monetary policies: money targeting, nominal-income targeting, real-GNP-plus-inflation targeting, and exchange rate targeting.[4] The policymakers for each country represented separately in a particular model were presumed to implement one of these national operating regimes, and the world combination of those national regimes constituted an international regime environment in the sense of this book. For the purposes of the project, countries in the European Monetary System other than Germany were treated differently from non-EMS countries such as the United States, Japan, and Canada; the non-German EMS countries were assumed to use their monetary-policy instrument to target their bilateral exchange rates against the deutsche-mark. Exchange rate targeting as specified for the project evoked the main features of the Bretton Woods system. Non-EMS countries and Germany were assumed to target their nominal bilateral exchange rate against the U.S. dollar, while model groups were asked to treat the United States as targeting its own money supply independently of exchange rates.

This particular project was stimulated in part by three papers presented at a December 1988 conference; each of those studies explored the use of stochastic simulation techniques to evaluate alternative monetary-policy regimes.[5] A few other papers with exploratory research on rule analysis of international regimes have also appeared in the technical literature.[6] Another strand of the literature relevant

---

4. The four simplified regimes are named after the right-hand-side variable(s) that serve as intermediate targets for policy. The target variable for money targeting was a narrowly defined monetary aggregate. The target variable for nominal-income targeting was the level of nominal GNP (the product of the price level and the level of real GNP). For real-GNP-plus-inflation, the target variable was the unweighted sum of two variables, the level of real GNP and the percent rate of change of the price level (GNP deflator). Real-GNP-plus-inflation targeting focuses on the *inflation rate*, whereas the price component of the target in nominal-income targeting is the *level* of prices. The target variable in exchange-rate targeting was a country's nominal bilateral exchange rate vis-à-vis the U.S. dollar.

5. See Frenkel, Goldstein, and Masson (1989); John Taylor (1989); and McKibbin and Sachs (1989).

6. Currie and Levine (1985); John Taylor (1988); Frenkel, Goldstein, and Masson (1990); Levine, Currie, and Gaines (1989); McKibbin and Sachs (1988, 1991); and Frankel and Chinn (1993).

here has been sparked by the extended target-zone proposal of John Williamson and Marcus Miller.[7]

Emphasis on Exchange Rates?

Apart from the studies mentioned in the preceding section, discussions of presumptive guidelines for international regimes have not struggled with the issues in an explicit general-equilibrium framework. Instead, commentary has typically focused attention only on exchange rates, exchange-rate targeting, and exchange-market intervention. For their part, policymakers appear to have made exchange rates the principal focus of international cooperation—or, at least, the rhetoric of cooperation—in the late 1980s and early 1990s.

That exclusive focus of attention on exchange rates seems to me misplaced. To be sure, I share with many economists the sense that exchange rates can be buffeted by excessive volatility or become misaligned transitorily, hence straying away from values consistent with fundamental economic determinants. I too believe that private exchange-market participants could benefit from having a more solid analytical anchor for their expectations about future exchange rates.[8] But I feel even more strongly that it is a mistake to become preoccupied with the exchange rate aspects of an international regime. The domestic-monetary and the fiscal aspects of national operating regimes are more important. Without an internally consistent specification of all aspects of an international regime, moreover, there are good reasons to doubt that any effort at aggressive management of exchange rates can be successful.

From the perspective of a single nation's policymakers, there is no logically valid dividing line between the external and domestic aspects of operating regimes for monetary policy and no way of compartmentalizing the external and domestic impacts of fiscal actions. Internationally agreed presumptive guidelines—traffic regulations—that apply exclusively to exchange rates or external reserves are thus bound to be

7. Williamson and Miller (1987); Williamson (1993); Williamson and Henning (1994); Bergsten and Williamson (1994). Efforts to study the target-zone regime environment include Edison, Miller, and Williamson (1987); Currie and Wren-Lewis (1989a, 1989b, 1990); Hughes Hallett, Holtham, and Hutson (1989); and Nedde (1989).

8. Bryant (1987a); Holtham (1989b); and Currie, Holtham, and Hughes Hallett 1989).

analytically unsound. Guidelines may exist that can make an international regime successful, but they will have to encompass the instruments, once thought to be "domestic," of national monetary and fiscal policies.

This basic point about international regimes is recognized in the most prominent academic proposals for presumptive guidelines.[9] It is less clear that policymakers themselves have adequately acknowledged the point in their intergovernmental bargaining about the management of exchange rates.

The limited empirical evidence available, at least as I read it, does not show exchange-rate targeting to be a promising international regime environment. One of the robust generalizations emerging from the research described in *Evaluating Policy Regimes* was the relatively poor performance of exchange-rate targeting relative to the other international regimes studied.[10] For most types of shocks, either real-GNP-plus-inflation targeting or nominal-income targeting outperformed both money targeting and exchange-rate targeting in stabilizing national economies when policymakers were assumed to stress real ultimate targets such as output or employment, or when they were assumed to stress a combination of such real variables and nominal ultimate targets (the inflation rate or the price level). This ranking was evident in a large majority of the cases studied in the theoretical analysis, in nearly three-fourths of the many deterministic simulations run for the ten models, and in more than five-sixths of the stochastic simulations.

The better overall performance of real-GNP-plus-inflation targeting and nominal-income targeting was admittedly less clear-cut for productivity and other supply shocks and for certain assumptions about the relative importance that policymakers attach to various ultimate-target variables. For example, the theoretical analysis suggested, and the two types of empirical simulation tended to confirm, that money targeting or exchange-rate targeting could be the preferred regime under one or (especially) both of two conditions: (1) if productivity or other supply shocks are the most prevalent disturbances to economies, and (2) if policymakers place great weight on

9. See, for example, Williamson and Miller (1987); McKinnon (1984, 1988); and Frankel (1990).

10. For a fuller summary of the generalizations in this and the next paragraph, see Bryant, Hooper, and Mann (1993, chap. 1).

stabilization of the inflation rate or the price level and place little or no weight on stabilization of output or employment. The project also found that, if policymakers placed significant weight on dampening the variability of financial variables such as interest rates and exchange rates, the case for preferring real-GNP-plus-inflation targeting and nominal-income targeting became still less strong, and could conceivably be overturned. Interest rates and exchange rates tended to be *more* variable under those two regimes, especially under real-GNP-plus-inflation targeting.

By reporting these negative results about exchange-rate targeting, I do not imply that the *Evaluating Policy Regimes* project produced a definitive reading. A minority of the participating model groups could not implement exchange-rate targeting in the form requested. The EMS was taken into account in only a rudimentary way. Most important, the project focused only on simple rules for national *monetary* policies, not on the combined functioning of monetary-policy and fiscal-policy operating regimes.

At a minimum, however, these extensive empirical experiments place a greater onus on the proponents of exchange-rate targeting as an international regime to come up with evidence that such an international regime is likely to have welfare-improving effects for individual countries and for the world as a whole. One can also interpret the turbulent EMS experience in September 1992 and July 1993 as raising anew questions about the dynamic stability of exchange-rate targeting. Such questions were rarely addressed in the European context during the four to five years preceding September 1992. The empirical assessment of the extended target-zone proposal conducted by David Currie and Simon Wren-Lewis, using the GEM model of the National Institute for Economic and Social Research in London, suggested that policy cooperation based on those presumptive guidelines would have led to substantial welfare gains for the G-3 countries (United States, Germany, and Japan) *relative to historical experience* from the mid-1970s to mid-1980s.[11] But even Currie and Wren-Lewis stress that much additional work evaluating the proposal needs to be carried out. Hughes Hallett's analysis of exchange-rate targeting reinforces this judgment.[12]

11. Currie and Wren-Lewis (1990).
12. See Hughes Hallett (1992). Eichengreen (1992, 1994); Eichengreen and Wyplosz (1993); Williamson (1993); and Goldstein, Folkerts-Landau, and others (1993) analyze the EMS experience of September 1992.

The preceding paragraphs focus on the stabilizing properties of alternative international regimes. To repeat, a balanced and complete rule analysis would have to offer satisfactory answers to all the questions raised earlier in this chapter. In particular, policymakers need sound advice about the likely trade-off between the stabilizing properties and the commitment properties of alternative international regimes and how best to choose an appropriate point on that trade-off curve.

Chapter 5

Cooperation and Coordination as Regime Maintenance and Satisficing Stabilization

A S SEEN BY proponents of simple rules, the major difficulty with policy-optimization analysis is its presumption in favor of discretionary activism. I now turn to quite different criticisms of policy optimization that have led other analysts to adopt an institutionalist perspective. These other critics wish to emphasize aspects of international cooperation that may be labeled "satisficing stabilization" and "maintenance of the international regime environment" ("regime maintenance" for short).

Institutionalist analysts regard policy optimization as tied to unrealistic or misleading assumptions and, therefore, not likely to be feasible in practice. One objection asserts that policy optimization fails to focus sufficiently on the management of crisis situations. A second line of criticism attacks the unitary-actor assumption as implausible and thus views the conclusions reached by policy-optimization analysis as lacking operational relevance. A third class of objections turns on issues of uncertainty, claiming that policy-optimization analysis often ignores uncertainty about countries' macroeconomic interactions and thereby fails to focus on the issues of international cooperation that national governments actually face. A final group of critics—especially noneconomists—argues that policy optimization takes too many institutional aspects as being exogenously given, with the result that it overlooks or downplays important dimensions of international cooperation. These last critics see policy optimization as paying little attention to international regimes and other important institutional aspects of cooperation.

Peter Kenen stresses a distinction between a "policy-optimizing approach" and a "regime-preserving approach" to international policy coordination. In describing the latter (where "regime" means "international regime environment" in my terminology), Kenen emphasizes its reliance on "mutual persuasion" in contrast to the "adversarial bargaining" of policy optimization. The regime-preserving approach, he writes, is concerned with "defend[ing] the international economic system from economic and political shocks, including misbehavior by governments themselves."[1] Institutionalist analysis, as I identify it, is broader than Kenen's regime-preserving approach, and it draws explicitly on the literature on international relations.[2]

Management of Crisis Situations

The perception that an international regime may be threatened by occasional crises, involving extreme turbulence in financial and economic transactions or in political interactions, arises naturally from historical experience. Episodes of turbulence have been common. International cooperation has not been so extensive and ingrained that it can be taken for granted by national governments. Actual international regimes, to the limited degree that they have existed, have been a fragile nexus of principles, norms, and decisionmaking procedures around which expectations can converge.

International cooperation, when most manifest, has often arisen in response to shared perceptions of a crisis.[3] Starting from this observation, one might claim that most international cooperation is best

---

1. Kenen (1990, p. 69).

2. My reasons for highlighting institutionalist analysis and regime maintenance are similar to Kenen's reasons for stressing regime preservation. Goldstein and Isard (1992); Masson (1992); and Ghosh and Masson (1994) echo the notion of regime preservation. Kenen cites Cooper (1986) and Kindleberger (1986) as economists writing in the vein of a regime-preserving approach. And he places Putnam and Bayne (1984, chap. 1) in this tradition as well, quoting their remark that "public goods must be produced and institutional arrangements defended by common or collective action." Fischer (1990b) in commenting on Kenen (1990, p. 70) describes the distinction between regime-preserving and policy-optimizing coordination as "suggestive but elusive," asks for more clarity about the regime that is allegedly being preserved, and expresses doubt about the usefulness of the distinction in debates about national policies.

3. Pauly (1992).

explained as actual or latent crisis management. A key part of this idea is the presumption that an existing international regime is valued by national governments (and at one remove by their citizens), even if national policymakers cannot readily demonstrate how the regime is beneficial in each and every circumstance. If this framework of international comity is threatened—if it looks as though major disruptions might cause one or more governments to act so as to undermine the international regime—then high priority is given to rallying round in the crisis.

The argument can be carried further. If national governments feel a need to maintain readiness to deal with possible future disruptions, then it may even be possible to interpret the ongoing intergovernmental consultations held in normal (noncrisis) periods as preparation for or insurance against latent crises. Without the regular, noncrisis consultations and without the bonding and sense of mutual confidence to which they give rise, the policymakers in national governments might be significantly less able to act effectively if and when actual crises materialize. During his tenure as economic counsellor at the International Monetary Fund, Jacob Frenkel frequently made this point by invoking the analogy of firefighters lounging about the firehouse playing cards in noncrisis times. Their apparent nonproductiveness cannot be appropriately judged unless one also takes into account their behavior when a fire has to be put out promptly.

The worldwide stock market crash of October 1987 illustrates the importance of uncertainty in financial markets for international cooperation. Paul Masson and Rex Ghosh examine this episode, emphasizing the extreme uncertainty about portfolio preferences in that crisis period as a powerful catalyst for policymakers.[4] In such a crisis in financial markets, they argue, policies are more likely to be influenced by shared goals. One can interpret their analysis of the 1987 crisis, I believe, as suggestively reinforcing the idea that crisis threats to the international regime and cooperative responses to them are critical features of international cooperation on national macroeconomic policies.[5]

---

4. Masson (1992); and Ghosh and Masson (1994, chap. 4).

5. The crisis-management aspects of international cooperation have been emphasized to me by Mitsuhiro Fukao in conversation and correspondence.

The Unitary-Actor Assumption of
Policy-Optimization Analysis

Consider next the assumption, typical of policy optimization, that each national government can be analytically treated as a unitary actor. Economists use this abstraction in virtually all prescriptive theory of economic policy, even when international aspects are ignored. Yet the concept of a single, unified policy authority and the consequent assumption of an integrated approach to macroeconomic policy within each national government are false representations of the political and bureaucratic facts of life. In all nations, the ship of state has many captains, and policy decisions are far from fully integrated. With a multiplicity of domestic agents pulling and pushing against one another, only a big stretch of the imagination allows one to see the national government as a unitary actor with a well-defined national loss function.

All theory must do violence to reality. Lack of realism is thus not by itself a damaging criticism of the traditional theoretical approach to economic policy and international cooperation. But the economists' practice of treating each national government as a unitary actor is open to criticism on a more fundamental point: this abstraction has inhibited thoughtful analytical study of the within-nation politics of macroeconomic policy. According to some critics, these domestic politics are so crucial as to render misleading the unitary-actor policy-optimization analysis that ignores them.[6]

Various types of institutionalist analysis pay much more explicit attention to domestic politics. Approaches emphasizing organizational process focus on the institutional forms and procedures of the individual agencies composing the national government. Models of governmental or bureaucratic politics emphasize the different perceptions, motivations, and powers of those agencies and the results of bargaining among them. More broadly still, other approaches encompass domestic actors outside as well as inside the national government and focus on the interrelationships among all the actors.[7]

6. For example, Putnam and Henning (1989, p. 106) remark that "the right question is not whether the unitary-actor assumption is unrealistic, but whether it is misleading. Unfortunately, we believe that it is the latter."

7. Jerry Cohen has emphasized the variety of approaches to domestic politics in the literatures on political science and international relations and has criticized my treatment of

Robert Putnam and Randall Henning, addressing the deficiencies of the unitary-actor model as they perceive them, introduce the idea of international economic policy coordination as a "two-level game":

> Games at both the domestic and international level are played simultaneously, so that national policies are in some sense the result of both the domestic and international parallelograms of forces. . . . Each national political leader appears at both game boards. Across the international table sit his foreign counterparts, and at his elbows sit diplomats and other international advisers. Around the domestic table behind him sit party and parliamentary figures, spokesmen for the great domestic ministries, representatives of key domestic interest groups, and the leader's own political advisers. . . . The special complexity of this two-level game is that moves that are rational for a player at one board . . . may be quite irrational for that same player at the other board. . . . Any key player at the international table who is dissatisfied with the outcome may upset the game board. Conversely, any national leader who fails to satisfy an adequate number of his fellow players at the domestic table risks being evicted from his seat.

Applying these ideas in a study of the 1978 Bonn economic summit, Putnam and Henning assert that "this two-table metaphor captures the dynamics of the 1977–78 negotiations better than any model based on unitary national actors."[8]

Seen from an institutionalist perspective, satisficing stabilization may be a more appropriate label for what is sought and sometimes achieved in international cooperation about national macroeconomic policies. Rather than attempting policy optimization through activist, full coordination, governments composed of many heterogeneous actors may have to settle for a satisficing second best that, although

---

these approaches as incomplete and inadequate. In Cohen (1990, pp. 268–70), he discusses the "levels-of-analysis issue" in political science; one of these levels of analysis (the "second image," or unit level) focuses on the roles of heterogeneous domestic politics and institutions.

   8. Putnam and Henning (1989); the quotations are from pp. 111–12. The two-table game metaphor is discussed in Putnam (1988). The concept originated, Henning has told me, in a 1986 Putnam-Henning draft of their essay published in 1989. For earlier illustrations of different institutionalist approaches, see Allison's study of the Cuban missile crisis (1971, especially chaps. 3–5); Simon (1959); March and Simon (1958); Steinbruner (1974); Halperin with Clapp and Kanter (1974); and Katzenstein (1978).

less precise, is also more attainable and less politically contentious. From an analytical perspective, the goal of this approach is to develop theoretical and historical explanations that take into account the (simultaneous) interactions of domestic and international decision-making.

Other Criticisms Generated by Institutionalist Analysis

Institutionalist analysis takes issue not only with the unitary-actor assumptions of policy optimization but also with several of its other simplifying assumptions. As before, the relevant question is whether those assumptions are productive or misleading, not whether they are realistic. Many analysts in international relations believe that policy optimization does have too narrow a focus and fails to consider important institutional aspects of international cooperation, which thereby render its conclusions misleading or at least only partially illuminating.

One point of departure for these critics is that state-centered, unitary-actor theories in economics and international relations "build very little sociality into their premises" and hence "are of limited value in explaining multilateral cooperation." Such theories, summarizes Caporaso, underestimate

the extent to which cooperation depends on a prior set of unacknowledged claims about the embeddedness of cooperative habits, shared values, and taken-for-granted rules. Further, its assumption that preferences are exogenously given reduces multilateralism to a question of strategic interaction, making it difficult to comprehend multilateralism propelled by collective beliefs, presumptive habits, and shared values. . . . Reflectivists [a label in international relations for some of the proponents of institutionalist analysis] reject the state of nature as the appropriate starting point even for heuristic purposes. If states are characterized only by interests and strategies, cooperative outcomes will not occur. Shared understandings regarding the rules of the game, the nature of permissible plays, the linkages between choices and outcomes, and the nature of agents involved in the game are important preconditions. To say this is to acknowledge that shared under-standings and communicative rationality are as important as in-strumental rationality.[9]

A socio-communicative approach, while retaining a focus on the identities and powers of individual nation-states, puts greater empha-sis on communication, persuasion, deliberation, and self-reflection in the "interaction repertoires" of states. A thoroughgoing institutional-ist approach highlights communication, discussion, and learning as well yet does not treat national preferences as exogenously given and does not try to interpret social relations solely as products of individ-ual self-interested calculations.

The flavor of socio-communicative and institutionalist views is well captured in another quotation from Caporaso's survey article on multilateralism. Institutionalism is preoccupied with the relationships among preferences, norms, beliefs, and institutions and aspires to "rethink the conventional relationships":

Conventional rational choice models in neoclassical economics start with exogenous preferences, a given distribution of endow-ments, and a given technology. The behavior of agents is explained by showing that they are responsive to changes in costs and bene-fits at the margin. In the institutional approach, however, norms, beliefs, and rules occupy a more central position. Individuals come to politics not only with preferences for particular outcomes but also with shared and divisive values and variously developed beliefs about the political process. . . . politics and individual preferences undergo change: not only do individuals 'act out' their preferences politically, but . . . the political process is a forum within which their preferences and beliefs change "as in the rest of life, through a combination of education, indoctrination, and experiences."[10]

9. Caporaso (1992, pp. 630–31). This survey of different approaches in the literature on international relations is helpful, and I have based some of my comments on Caporaso's analysis.

10. Caporaso (1992, pp. 624–25). The quotation within the quotation is from March and Olsen (1984, p. 739). In addition to March and Olsen, Caporaso cites Keohane (1988) and Powell and DiMaggio (1991) as overviews of a growing literature on institutionalism. This literature has links to the new institutionalism in neoclassical economics (associated, for example, with Oliver Williamson and Douglas North) that highlights principal-agent issues and transactions costs. Other researchers contributing to the institutionalist literature in international relations include Ernst Haas, John Ruggie, Hayward Alker, Richard Ashley, Judith Goldstein, and Alexander Wendt.

Policy optimization and institutionalism tend to have analogously contrasting interpretations of historical experience. Traditional economic theory predicts outcomes, including institutional outcomes, largely on the basis of choice-theoretic efficiency (with given preferences, technology, and endowments). In contrast, the institutionalist perspective emphasizes the contingent, path-dependent nature of institutional change.[11] Institutions are analyzed as changing environments within which actors, including national governments, learn to alter perceptions of their interests and beliefs.

Diffuse reciprocity is the notion that each nation engaging in international cooperation expects to benefit over many periods on many issues, not necessarily to benefit in every period on every issue. The emphasis on diffuse reciprocity is another characteristic that differentiates institutionalism from policy optimization.[12] If one thinks in terms of the concepts of Albert Hirschman, there is much more emphasis on "voice" in institutionalist analysis than on "exit" (exit interpreted broadly to mean that a nation "will not play the game" unless the game will yield good outcomes judged by the benchmark of the national loss function).[13] In terms of the concepts of Jon Elster and Anatol Rapoport, respectively, the institutionalists give more attention to forum than to market and more often define situations as debates than as fights or games.[14]

A Preliminary Assessment

How much weight should economists accord to the institutionalist perspective? At the very least, the institutionalist criticisms should caution one not to lose sight of the extreme nature of some of the analytical abstractions that economists employ. There is great force in the contention that unitary-actor analysis of national government decisions may be misleading. Focusing on the multiplicity of agents and forces within a national government—the juxtaposition of a domestic bargaining table with the international game board—reinforces the conclusion that international cooperation becomes more difficult as

11. Caporaso (1989, 1992).
12. Krasner (1983a, p. 3); and Keohane (1986).
13. Hirschman (1970).
14. Elster (1986); and Rapoport (1960).

the number of interacting agents increases (and hence is an order of magnitude more difficult than it is made to appear when national governments are treated as unitary actors). Similarly, the crisis-management line of reasoning merits further careful attention by economists.

My conjecture is that the varieties of institutionalist analysis, when developed further and applied thoughtfully, will generate many more insights. I do not know the relevant literatures sufficiently well, however, to be able to give institutionalist ideas a detailed appraisal. And I have only tentative views about how best to use these ideas to modify conclusions reached in the economics literature.

Perhaps because I am unable to wriggle far enough out of the straitjacket of my economics training, I am reluctant to rely on institutionalist analysis as a substitute for the policy-optimization perspective. But of course no compelling reason exists to treat the two as substitutes rather than complements. The insights from each can be combined to generate a balanced and more thoughtful understanding.

At its best, furthermore, policy-optimization analysis can be made more flexible. By thoughtfully amending some of its assumptions or casting its net more widely, it can be extended to tackle some of the issues emphasized in institutional analysis. We have surely not learned all we can by operating with the "as if" assumptions that nations have well-defined loss functions and act to optimize their decisions accordingly. For example, it may be possible to creatively adapt national loss functions to include variables that represent some of the diversity of domestic politics or that capture some aspects of the international regime that nations regard as shared goals. Institutionalist critics should also acknowledge that economists' analyses of repeated games, reputation, and credibility are aimed at the very phenomena that institutionalists wish to discuss under the heading of diffuse reciprocity.

Policy-optimization analysis can also take into account uncertainty of various types. Indeed, traditional economic analysis has probably done more to incorporate the consequences of uncertainty into its conclusions than have the institutionalist critics who assert the importance of uncertainty but have not taken many steps to study it analytically.

Chapter 6

Can Coordination Be Counterproductive?

FROM TIME TO time several arguments have been advanced claiming that efforts to cooperate internationally can have undesirable consequences. Activist coordination, in particular, attracts this reaction. This chapter summarizes and evaluates such criticisms.

Do Coordination Efforts Create Inappropriate Incentives?

One line of argument asserts that efforts to cooperate are not desirable because they may deflect the attention of national governments from higher-priority (domestic) policy choices or give governments incentives to delay policy actions they ought to be taking regardless of international considerations. Some analysts even see international negotiations and bargaining as a smokescreen, enabling a government to blame foreigners for its own failure to take responsible action.

Most critics adopting this position seem to be primarily worried about international efforts to achieve activist coordination. Few seem to object to some degree of ongoing consultations and exchanges of information. As far as I know, moreover, such critics do not object to the crisis-management cooperation emphasized by institutionalist analysts (although they might be uncomfortable with a low-threshold definition of "crisis" that made it too easy for governments to invoke the crisis-management rationale).

Herbert Stein, Max Corden, Jacques Polak, and Roland Vaubel are articulate examplars of a skeptical view. Stanley Fischer should probably be classified as a partial doubter.[1] The most prominent critic of the usefulness of activist coordination has been Martin Feldstein. In several publications following his service as chairman of the U.S. Council of Economic Advisers, Feldstein stressed that, although he was not opposed to international cooperation in economic affairs and that (activist) coordination could sometimes be appropriate for individual countries, "Many of the claimed advantages of cooperation and coordination are wrong," "There are substantial risks and disadvantages to the types of coordination that are envisioned," "An emphasis on coordination can distract attention from the necessary changes in domestic policy," "The United States is particularly unsuited to participate in an ongoing process of economic coordination," and "An emphasis on international interdependence instead of sound domestic policies makes foreign governments the natural scapegoats for any poor economic performance."[2]

In his study for this Integrating National Economies series, Robert Paarlberg picks up the themes stressed by Feldstein and applies them to U.S. choices about fiscal policy. Paarlberg argues, like Feldstein, that efforts at international coordination in the 1980s tended to give timid U.S. policymakers additional excuses for deferring needed reductions in the large federal budget deficit. Paarlberg interprets activist coordination of fiscal policies as an example of "outward-oriented" U.S. policy action, in contrast to the "inward-oriented" approach he believes superior.[3]

I have never been able to regard this line of criticism as compelling. Individual government leaders, administrators, and members of parliaments are undoubtedly capable of short-sighted behavior. Policymakers of one nation can be tempted to deflect attention from difficult issues and choices by invoking foreign pressures or external constraints on policies. Examples can be cited for most nations. The United States is an especially fertile source for illustrations.

But short-sighted or obfuscating behavior can—and does—occur over any issue, domestic or international. Policymakers frequently have their attention deflected by domestic red herrings from neces-

1. Stein (1978, 1987); Corden (1983, 1986, also 1994); Polak (1981, 1991); Vaubel (1983, 1985); and Fischer (1988).

2. M. Feldstein, "The End of Policy Coordination," *Wall Street Journal,* November 9, 1987, p. A26. See also (1988a, 1988b, pp. 3, 4, 12).

3. Paarlberg (1995, pp. 57–66).

sary policy actions. Possibilities for distracted attention or obfuscation are seldom invoked as a valid rationale for discouraging a government from pursuing one or another domestic objective. Why should international objectives be regarded as so different?

If international cooperation, including activist coordination, can offer opportunities for a nation to benefit significantly, provided the cooperation is pursued thoughtfully and without obfuscation, why should the risk of deflected priorities be used as an argument against the international cooperation? The remedy for the risk of deflected priorities is to try to straighten out the erring policymakers rather than choose to forgo the benefits of cooperation. The situation is analogous to the risks that doctors run when prescribing medications that must be wisely used. The risk that some patients may swallow an entire bottle of aspirin is not accepted as a valid reason for urging the doctors not to prescribe aspirin at all.

Feldstein implies, misleadingly in my view, that proponents of coordination recommend international cooperation *instead* of sound domestic policies. Sound domestic policies should always—it scarcely needs saying—be preferred to unsound domestic policies. The real issue is whether or not efforts at international coordination can facilitate the selection of mutually sound domestic policies, by all nations participating in the coordination, thereby favorably supplementing what domestic policies would otherwise have been.

Paarlberg argues that appropriate macroeconomic policies should be implemented *prior* to any efforts at international coordination. Paarlberg's distinction between outward-first coordination and inward-first policy development, however, seems a bit strained to me. In general, I fail to see why a national government cannot simultaneously look inward and outward, trying to proceed on both fronts in a complementary way. Again, if thoughtfully pursued, coordination efforts need not accede to, or generate, inappropriate incentives.[4]

The potential weakness in my argument here—the germ of truth in this line of criticism—is embedded in the premise "if thoughtfully

4. Paarlberg observes that his outward-first leadership might be the more appropriate approach for the United States in some issue areas, but he argues that his inward-first approach will normally be preferred, especially for macroeconomic policies. Although I believe that Paarlberg's distinction between U.S. leadership styles is overdrawn and hence at times constrains his analysis in a straitjacket, his book contains many useful insights into U.S. foreign economic policy.

pursued." There can be no guarantee that international coordination will be pursued thoughtfully. When it is not, the results in some circumstances can certainly prove counterproductive.

Consider the success in reducing inflation during the 1980s of countries participating in the European Monetary System. This episode has often been cited as an illustration (for the European region) of successful policy coordination. The literature correctly emphasizes that this success can be traced in large part to the fact that the economically and politically most powerful country in the EMS, Germany, itself had a very low inflation rate. The less powerful EMS countries were thus induced to follow monetary policies that became progressively more consistent with the policy of the German Bundesbank. Those countries anchored themselves to Germany and thereby bought credibility for their monetary policies. But suppose, suggests Vito Tanzi, that Italy rather than Germany had been the major economic power in Europe when the EMS was launched. Given the high Italian inflation rate and Italy's monetary policy at that time, one could imagine that other European countries would have adjusted their monetary policies in an expansionary direction to conform, at least in part, to Italian policy. The outcome could have been a markedly higher long-run rate of inflation and less credible, more costly anti-inflation policies.[5]

Coordinating behavior of the sort in this hypothetical example is labeled by Tanzi as the fox-without-the-tail syndrome, after Aesop's fable in which the fox that has lost his tail tries to convince other foxes that a tail is a burden and that they would be better off if they too cut their tails off. Tanzi believes that the syndrome may be pertinent for international efforts to coordinate fiscal policies:

> International coordination of fiscal policy inevitably creates pressures on those countries that have been more successful in recent years in correcting their fiscal imbalances to relax their fiscal policy to bring it more in line with that of countries where less adjustment has taken place. These pressures on the former will become stronger the less successful are the latter in putting their fiscal houses in order. If these pressures succeeded, fiscal coordination might not generate *over the medium run* the desirable results, even if

5. Tanzi (1989, pp. 25–26).

it succeeded in bringing some short-run stimulation to aggregate demand.[6]

Thoughtful Europeans have worried that the fox-without-a-tail syndrome has from time to time surfaced in internal bargaining in the European Union. The most egregious examples, it is often claimed, can be seen in decisions about the Common Agricultural Policy. Analogous criticisms have occasionally been made about the G-7 summit meetings. If I believed that the fox-without-a-tail syndrome were characteristic of most intergovernmental discussions about macro-economic policies, or that latent tendencies of this type could easily go undetected, I would align myself with Stein-Corden-Feldstein skepticism. On the whole, however, I do not perceive the virus as wide-spread. Nor do I think it easily escapes detection when it does infect individual governments.

Does Coordination Injure Third Parties?

A different line of argument asserts that international cooperation, especially activist coordination, can reduce rather than increase welfare if a subgroup of agents cooperates in the absence—and without regard for the interests—of relevant third parties. The excluded third parties might be national governments not participating in inter-governmental bargaining. Or those excluded might be private citizens of the nations whose governments were cooperating in a fashion incompatible with the citizens' true interests.

Kenneth Rogoff articulated this line of criticism in an influential article identifying circumstances in which activist coordination be-tween two national governments could actually reduce welfare for the nations' residents.[7] The underlying mechanism causing this result in Rogoff's theoretical model is the exclusion of the world private sector from the coordinating bargain. In effect, one of the key players in the game-theoretic situation is not permitted at the bargaining table, and the outcome that results from the bargaining does not reflect that player's interests. When the two governments in Rogoff's model do

6. Tanzi (1989, p. 26, emphasis in original). Paarlberg (1995, p. 61) quotes this view of Tanzi approvingly.

7. Rogoff (1985a).

not coordinate their policies, each government is constrained because of a knowledge that a monetary expansion will depreciate its currency (the exchange rate in the model is flexible) and thereby cause higher inflation. In effect, the noncooperative solution restrains temptation for the central banks. If the two governments are permitted to coordinate their policy actions, however, a joint monetary expansion will not lead to a depreciation of either currency, and the restraint that prevents the central banks from pursuing overly expansionary policies is removed. But the forward-looking agents in the private sector understand that international coordination removes the restraint on temptation and raise their wage demands accordingly. The coordination outcome thus produces higher inflation and reduces welfare relative to noncoordination.

Matthew Canzoneri and Dale Henderson study coalitions in which two governments cooperate but interact strategically (play a noncooperative Nash game rather than cooperate) with a third government. They point out that the results of two-party game analyses "can either overstate or understate the gains from cooperation if third-party reactions are being ignored," and indeed (like Rogoff) that "cooperation may even be counterproductive."[8] Canzoneri and Henderson also emphasize, however, that seemingly paradoxical results about cooperation proving to be counterproductive need careful interpretation.

> It appears that whether cooperation can be counterproductive depends on the commitment technology available to the policymakers attempting to form a coalition. If the technology allows the policymakers to commit with respect to each other, but does not allow the coalition to commit with respect to third parties, then examples of counterproductive cooperation are easy to come by. However, we think that these examples are incomplete until the commitment technology is actually specified. For if, at the opposite extreme, the technology that supports cooperation between the policymakers also allows the coalition to commit with respect to third parties, then the coalition becomes a Stackelberg leader. In this case, cooperation could never be counterproductive, since the coalition could always choose to play the old Nash equilibrium

8. Canzoneri and Henderson (1991, p. 6).

policies. Those who worry that cooperation might be counterproductive should specify a mechanism that allows commitment between coalition members but not between the coalition and third
parties if their examples are to be taken seriously.[9]

Numerous other papers in the literature have explored cooperative
solutions to games that decrease rather than increase welfare.[10]

Market Failures and Government Failures Once Again

The studies referred to in the preceding sections adopt a game-
theoretic perspective within the tradition of policy-optimization analysis. The argument that coordination efforts can be counterproductive
has been taken even further, and shifted into more explicitly political
territory, by some adherents of a "public choice" view of economics.
These public-choice analysts argue that governments are organizations with interests of their own, which are different from, and potentially inimical to, those of general populations. Consequently, these
analysts recommend that national governments be prevented from
"colluding" (their interpretation of international cooperation, especially activist coordination). Instead, they advocate intergovernmental
competition, not coordination, as being more likely to serve the
interests of general populations. Seen in the context of figure 2-3,
such critics favor mutual-recognition types of international regime, if
any international regime at all. Most also tend to be proponents of
simple rules rather than activist discretion, seeking to constrain the
authority of government officials as much as possible.[11]

The analytical arguments that intergovernmental cooperation and
coordination can produce undesirable outcomes for excluded parties,
including general populations, have to be taken seriously. Recall also
that intergovernmental exchanges of information have a potential not

---

9. Canzoneri and Henderson (1991, p. 74).

10. These other contributions include Miller and Salmon (1985); Kehoe (1986, 1989);
Currie, Levine, and Vidalis (1987); and Levine and Currie (1987). Carraro and Giavazzi
(1991) take issue with the Rogoff (1985a) model and provide a counterexample in which,
with three agents per economy (government, firms, and trade unions), cooperation is
welfare enhancing. Tabellini (1988) is also relevant.

11. James Buchanan is a noted expositor of the public-choice view; see, for example,
Brennan and Buchanan (1977, 1980).

only to enhance macroeconomic performance but possibly to reduce welfare by misleading or deceiving other governments and the public (chapter 3). These situations are particular cases of the assertion that "government failure" can have consequences worse than the "market failure" originally giving rise to, or used to justify, government intervention (chapter 2). Historians have no difficulties in finding numerous examples in real life of government failure within national polities and economies. Because governmental interactions across borders have been much less extensive than domestic governance, significant international examples are less readily identified. But such examples can no doubt be found.

Are government failures so prevalent that governments should be severely constrained from trying to remedy market failures? Is it the general case, or the occasional exception, when politicians and government officials pursue their personal, private interests in contradiction to the general welfare of the citizens in their jurisdiction? Answers to such questions are of course highly contingent on the nations or jurisdictions involved. The greater the transparency of government activities and the stronger the procedures for democratic accountability, the less likely it is that serious government failures will be widespread. Accountability and transparency in the largest OECD nations are less robust than one could wish. Even so, the levels are sufficiently high to permit major changes in local and national jurisdictions through periodic elections. For these nations, the actual state of affairs is a murky intermediate position between the extremes of governments that persistently malfunction and those that are highly accountable.

This intermediate murkiness applies to intergovernmental interactions no less than to domestic governance. The underlying rationale for intergovernmental cooperation is the correction of market failures stemming from spillover externalities. But the cooperation can sometimes be counterproductive because of government failure. What general proclivity, then, should a reasonable person have about efforts to cooperate?

On balance, I do not regard the arguments summarized in this chapter as persuasive grounds for generally eschewing efforts to cooperate or coordinate. For each of the different contexts and forums in which consultations and potential coordination are under consideration, a judgment has to be made about the greater danger: that collusion between governments will work against the collective interest; or, alternatively, that the absence of international cooperation will allow cross-border spillovers and externalities to work to the detriment of the collective interest. Governmental policy, for all its imperfections and potential for failure, is virtually the only vehicle that nations have to represent the collective purpose. If public goods and collective action are sometimes necessary, then governments are necessary, and this proposition carries over to the international domain. The premise underlying my personal views is that, on the whole, international cooperation among governments, especially democratically elected governments, can plausibly be expected—in many, though admittedly not all, circumstances—to further the collective interests of their citizens.[12]

The presumption of subsidiarity (chapter 2), if broadly accepted, offers a bit of protection against overly zealous efforts to cooperate and against abuse of such efforts as are implemented. Activist coordination, in particular, would be attempted only when accumulating evidence points to the existence of spillover externalities and to a feasible mutual adjustment of national policies that seem likely to yield a significantly better outcome.

---

12. Other papers that share this political premise include Frenkel, Goldstein, and Masson (1989); Artis and Ostry (1986); Dobson (1991, 1994); and Solomon (1991). Bryant (1987a, 1990b) has more discussion of the political background to international cooperation.

Chapter 7

The Implications of Uncertainty

EVEN ANALYSTS who want national governments to try to cooperate acknowledge that such efforts may not be feasible. The fundamental obstacles to feasibility are various types of uncertainty. In real-life circumstances, policymakers and analysts in a home nation are uncertain about, first, the current positions of the home and foreign economies—the so-called initial conditions and shocks that are currently buffeting those economies; second, the objectives and intentions of policymakers in other national governments—the loss functions that guide the policymakers' decisions; and, third, the actual functioning of the world economy, including especially how policy actions themselves influence the home and foreign economies—the analytical model that represents interactions within and among the national economies. All three aspects of uncertainty can have decisive consequences for international cooperation. I focus on the last two.

Uncertainty about National Objectives and Intentions

Even when analysts look through the lenses of game theory and policy optimization, uncertainty about the policymakers' loss functions can have an important bearing on analytical conclusions. Although the outside analyst is likely to assume correct knowledge of each player's loss function, the individual players themselves—the (unitary-actor) national governments—can be assumed to have only imperfect information about the others' functions. Such uncertainty leads naturally to issues of deception, bluffing, and reputation, and

74

hence to the consideration of reneging on agreements, of monitoring compliance with agreements (enforceability), and of the use of "trigger mechanisms" to facilitate enforceability.

From an institutionalist perspective, uncertainty about the objectives and intentions of national governments may be even more important. When it is acknowledged that each national government is composed of multiple agents interacting with one another—when the "domestic game board" is crowded and confusing—the issues of bluffing, deliberate deception, and willful reneging at the international game board will probably be less relevant. But the ability of national governments to make and effectively "deliver" on international agreements, and therefore also the problems of monitoring compliance, will have still greater salience.

Uncertainty about policymakers' objectives and intentions is thus a major stumbling block for international cooperation, and especially for activist coordination. A considerable part of the literature on policy optimization discusses this nexus of issues by emphasizing reneging, cheating, and the "sustainability" of cooperation. It is more revealing, in my opinion, to emphasize other aspects of uncertainty.

Reneging on an international agreement (defection) can be voluntary or involuntary.[1] Voluntary reneging is the deliberate decision of a rational agent to defect from an agreement because he expects to improve his strategic situation by doing so. Bluffing, deception, and apprehension about other agents' compliance may precede the decision. Voluntary reneging is typically studied under the assumption that national governments behave as if they were unitary actors. Involuntary reneging is a notion that stems from an institutionalist perspective on agreements. It occurs when an individual policymaker, being part of a national government that does *not* behave as a unitary actor, is unable to deliver on a previous promise.

Institutionalists tend to believe that game-theoretic economics has exaggerated the importance of voluntary reneging. Robert Putnam and Randall Henning, for example, find the concept unhelpful in studying the 1978 Bonn summit and argue that such behavior is much less common, particularly among Western democratic governments, than policy-optimization theorists would predict.[2] The institu-

---

1. This distinction is emphasized in Putnam and Henning (1989, pp. 99–102).
2. Putnam and Henning (1989).

tionalist presumption is that conditional cooperators in repeated games, concerned about their reputations and credibility and judging their participation in international cooperation by the standard of diffuse reciprocity, will hesitate to deceive or renege voluntarily for the purpose of capturing short-run advantages.

Much of the game theorists' emphasis on time consistency and trigger mechanisms also seems artificial to institutionalist analysts. For example, they doubt that real-life policymakers are so averse to "giving up some sovereignty" to a third-party monitor (such as an international institution) that they will search for a complex trigger mechanism as a substitute for third-party oversight.

My sympathies lie with the institutionalists on these points, largely because the policy-optimization perspective on reneging and compliance has paid too little attention to uncertainty. In real life, the multiple agents within national governments and all the private sector agents in their economies have too little information, of too low a quality, to identify reneging behavior.[3] Imagine the possibility of a government voluntarily reneging in period 2 on policies announced in period 1. What can reneging mean? In real life, it cannot plausibly mean that the government "re-optimizes" in period 2 and thus changes its instrument settings away from the preannounced settings that were derived from optimization calculations in period 1. Private sector agents and other governments should not rationally want the government to stick to a previously announced "open loop" path for its instruments if new disturbances have occurred in the meantime. Hence, the only logically sound notion of reneging must imply that the government announces in period 1 future paths for its instrument settings—in effect, a complex set of "closed loop" reaction-function equations—that are explicitly contingent on the occurrence of every conceivable type of future disturbance. Reneging must then be defined as a departure from these complex, reaction-function rules. Under this definition, however, the information presumed to be available to governments and private sector agents is enormously greater than what they actually have. The monitoring and signal-extraction abilities implicitly attributed to the other governments and private sector agents are thus implausible. Governments in practice do not design and announce policies as complex as these future-disturbance-

---

3. This paragraph repeats a point stressed in Bryant (1987b, pp. 11–12).

contingent rules. The concept of reneging that has received such attention in the game-theory literature, therefore, has limited practical applicability.[4]

Although an institutionalist perspective may downplay the importance of reneging, cheating, and willful deception, it will nonetheless assign great importance to issues of monitoring and "ability to deliver." Putnam and Henning, for example, argue that deliverability was a prominent feature of the negotiations for the 1978 Bonn summit, even though concern about cheating and reneging was not. "The Americans worked hard to convince the others, first, that [President Carter] was under severe domestic political constraints on energy issues that limited what he could promise, but, second, that he could deliver on what he was prepared to promise."[5]

Uncertainty about the objectives and intentions of national governments, about their ability to deliver on agreements, and about their ability to monitor the compliance of other governments, is a troublesome type of uncertainty that can undermine the feasibility of international cooperation. But it is not as consequential as the type of uncertainty I turn to next.

Uncertainty about the Functioning of the World Economy

Policymakers and their advisers have only limited knowledge about the functioning of their national economies. Their understanding of how national economies interact to generate global economic outcomes is still more imperfect. This analytical ignorance—for brevity, "model uncertainty"—is the single greatest impediment to sound policymaking within national governments and to successful international cooperation for macroeconomic policies.

Real-life policymaking is bedeviled by the competing-model problem. To formulate alternative courses of action and to clarify the likely costs and benefits associated with them, a decisionmaker (with the help of his or her advisers) must employ some sort of analytical model that connects policy actions to expected outcomes. But several rival

4. Note, however, the similarity to the analytical issues that have to be faced in specifying and evaluating the presumptive guidelines to be studied in the rule analysis of international regimes!

5. Putnam and Henning (1989, p. 105).

models will be available, often embodying significantly different analytical views and having conflicting implications for policy decisions. Basic disagreements exist, for example, about how to characterize the behavior of private economic agents, how to describe the behavior of policy authorities themselves, how to treat expectations of future economic developments, and what to assume about the current and future values of the driving forces not treated endogenously in a model. The decisionmaker will accordingly be uncertain which of the competing models represents the least inadequate approximation of the "true" model (the actual relationships that will in reality determine the consequences of policy actions).

When one focuses on the competing-model problem, it is helpful to distinguish among model construction, model evaluation, model improvement, and model selection. Model construction is the initial process of building some piece of analytical machinery to shed light on issues of interest. It typically involves numerous steps of theoretical refinement, specification of structure, and econometric estimation. Construction of a model or several alternative models is self-evidently a prerequisite for model evaluation and model improvement. Similarly, there is no competing-model problem facing a policymaker unless several different explicit models have already been constructed. I am concerned here with issues that postdate model construction.

Model evaluation systematically compares a model with the objectives for which it has been constructed and assesses its performance according to theoretical and economic criteria thought to be characteristic of a "good" model. Model evaluation can also entail systematic comparisons of the performance of alternative models. The process of model evaluation thus plays an essential role in identifying the relative strengths and weaknesses of competing models. Ideally, such evaluation pays special attention to the inadequacies of individual models and inconsistencies across models.[6]

---

6. Since the mid-1980s, the Brookings Institution, together with other organizations such as the Federal Reserve Board, the Centre for Economic Policy Research in London, the OECD, and the Korea Development Institute, has sponsored a series of international collaborative projects among model groups that have constructed empirical multicountry models. Model evaluation has been a primary objective of the projects. The resulting publications include Bryant and others (1988); Bryant, Holtham, and Hooper (1988); Hooper and others (1990); Bryant and others (1989); and Bryant, Hooper, and Mann (1993).

Model improvement attempts to remedy the inadequacies of individual models and to promote convergence among competing models. If the processes of model evaluation and model improvement worked ideally, inconsistencies across models would be gradually eliminated and a single model would become the encompassing, consensus model (for a particular analytical purpose).

Because the processes of model evaluation and improvement do not work ideally, policymakers are confronted with the thorny issues of model selection, that is, the competing-model problem proper. This problem presupposes that several alternative models have been constructed, all presumptively relevant to the analytical problem facing a policymaker. And it presupposes that model evaluation and model improvement have not yet produced a professional consensus on a single best model for the relevant purpose in hand.

Accumulation of robust empirical knowledge does not occur quickly, at least not in macroeconomics. The techniques of model evaluation are not sufficiently robust. Nor are the prospects for model improvement sufficiently good to permit policymakers to believe that macroeconomists will soon converge on a single, "true" model for any single economy, let alone for the global economy. Nor does it seem likely that macroeconomists will soon converge on a single model that encompasses its predecessors as special cases.

Both classical and Bayesian statistical theory rest on the hope that model evaluation and improvement will eventually lead to an encompassing model. But this hope may be forlorn. The true structure to be estimated may change over time (or, if one prefers, the true "deep" parameters that are time invariant cannot be identified and reliably estimated). Statistical theory presumes that a researcher can obtain a lengthy sample of data or draw repeatedly from the invariant true structure. In practical macroeconomics, however, the feasible samples may be small, measurements of data from periods far in the past may be relatively uninformative, and in any case data may be unavailable or, if available, measured with large errors. Statistical theory with its working assumptions can plausibly assert that modeling efforts are likely to converge to the true structure. But it is much less plausible to hold out a similar hope for macroeconomic modeling of national economies and their interactions.

The awkward fact is that policymakers in national governments will have to wait a very long time for model evaluators and model improvers to reach a degree of convergence sufficient to make the competing-model problem unimportant in practice. And it is excessively optimistic to believe that incorrect models can be convincingly rejected merely by reference to the data alone.

The competing claims of rival models and the other dimensions of model uncertainty would not vex policymakers greatly if policymakers could safely downplay uncertainty. But they cannot do so. In any practical policy situation, uncertainty should be explicitly taken into account in the course of formulating and implementing decisions.

Uncertainty about the consequences of a policymaker's own actions—about the time paths of the policy "multipliers" associated with the policymaker's instruments—is an especially critical type of uncertainty. In contrast with other forms of uncertainty for which it may sometimes be sensible to form expectations of the uncertain coefficients or variables and treat those expected values as if they were certain, policymakers should never ignore uncertainty about policy multipliers. Even if it were feasible to use policy doses of any size (which of course it is not), it would be inappropriate to select those instrument settings that would be dictated by focusing on the expected values of multipliers while ignoring their variances and covariances. All available instruments should be fully utilized, moreover, no matter how few the target variables that are the objective of policy and no matter how plentiful the instruments. As a general presumption, the more uncertain are its multipliers, the less aggressively should one use an individual policy instrument. More broadly stated, the greater the uncertainty associated with the policy multipliers, the less active policymakers should be in adjusting the settings of the corresponding instruments.[7]

Policymakers in a hypothetical, completely closed national economy would be confounded by numerous types of "domestic" uncertainty. But "international" uncertainties associated with the growing interdependence of national economies are often even more troublesome. Only limited analytical agreement exists about how policy

---

7. The basic reference for these generalizations is the seminal article by Brainard (1967). Many subsequent researchers have confirmed the importance of this line of inquiry. For applications to international cooperation, see among others Ghosh (1986); Ghosh and Ghosh (1991); Masson (1992); and Ghosh and Masson (1994). Bryant (1985) emphasized the importance of uncertainty issues.

actions and nonpolicy disturbances originating in one nation spill across borders to influence economic developments in other nations. For most nations, this lack of agreement is more pronounced than the disagreement among analysts about how individual national economies behave.

Increasing economic interdependence would substantially complicate policymaking even if governments had reliable estimates of the cross-border spillovers. Typically, larger cross-border spillovers reduce the effects of a country's policy instruments on its own national variables relative to their effects on variables in other countries, and hence reduce the autonomy of economic policy. Externally originating forces constrain the ability of a government to achieve its goals, thereby diminishing the control that a nation's policymakers can exert over own-nation target variables. The closer intertwining of economies renders policy decisions in any single nation more difficult.[8]

The difficulties for policy are magnified by great uncertainty about the empirical magnitudes, and sometimes even the directions, of the cross-border spillovers. A nation's policymakers know that policy actions and nonpolicy shocks originating abroad will constrain their own policy choices, and that their actions will alter outcomes and policy choices in other countries, but the forms and magnitudes cannot be well estimated. In such circumstances of enhanced uncertainty, appropriate decisionmaking becomes especially difficult.

These points bear powerfully on conclusions about international cooperation reached by way of the policy-optimization perspective. But they have the same importance for rule analysis and institutionalist analysis. All three perspectives share the presumption (albeit with different nuances) that national governments can sometimes foster their nations' interests by framing their policies cooperatively. But how can governments cooperate when they are so uncertain about how nations' actions influence one another? More of a consensus about the direction and size of cross-border interactions is a necessary—though far from sufficient—condition for significant progress in facilitating cooperation for national macroeconomic policies.

Is model uncertainty a valid reason for believing that international cooperation, especially activist coordination, may not be *desirable* (as opposed to being infeasible)? In a widely cited study, Jeffrey Frankel

8. Bryant (1980).

and Katherine Rockett appeared to answer yes to this question.[9] Frankel and Rockett (hereafter FR) drew on the extensive simulation experiments in the first Brookings comparative-model evaluation to calculate gains and losses from policy coordination for the United States and an aggregate constituting the rest of the OECD region (ROECD). Since multiplier estimates were available for ten models, the FR calculations were done for 1,000 possible combinations of assumptions.[10] For every conceivable pair of model choices by the two governments, the U.S. and the ROECD policymakers in FR's analysis were presumed to select adjustments in policy instruments they each believed would raise their own nation's welfare. FR concluded that such policy adjustments could in fact lower welfare as easily as raise it when the consequences of the adjustments were evaluated with a third model as the true model. The counting of cases was done in several different ways, but FR typically found that coordination was beneficial to both the United States and the ROECD in only some 50 to 65 percent of the possible combinations. Frankel subsequently summarized the research with remarks such as "coordination in the presence of model uncertainty can leave countries worse off ex post as easily as better off."[11]

Incontrovertibly, policymakers can lower welfare by using an incorrect model. And since no one can know with any confidence what the true model is, policymakers will inevitably make mistakes. As stressed already, however, policymakers necessarily rely on some form of analytical model. Models can be explicit and systematic. Or models can be casually, sometimes even carelessly, devised—or even implicitly presumed. Yet a model of *some* sort is a logical prerequisite for decisions on what to do with policy instruments. It would be foolish to assert that all existing models are so uncertain and unreliable that policymakers should avoid using any of them. Policymakers cannot realistically ignore all models. They cannot set all their policy instruments at "zero" values, so to speak, and decide to have no policy at all.

---

9. Frankel and Rockett (1988); see also Frankel (1988b).

10. Frankel and Rockett assumed that each of the two "governments" selects one of the ten models as its preferred model; alternative selections produce 100 possible model pairings. For every pairing, Frankel and Rockett assumed that each of the ten models is the "true" model. Hence the authors evaluated altogether 1,000 (= 10×100) combinations of assumptions.

11. Frankel (1989, p. 52).

If a policymaker chooses to ignore all explicit models, in essence he chooses to use an implicit model—which is typically still more flawed and unreliable than the explicit models. Explicit models can at least be analyzed, criticized, and improved. Implicit models can be badly wrong and can stay wrong because they are not subjected to criticism.

How, then, should one interpret the FR analysis? In my view, the authors overstate the pessimistic inferences drawn from their analysis. Unfortunately, many casual readers of their paper have gone still further astray in misrepresenting the inferences. Loosely, and wrongly in my view, the FR analysis has been cited as strong evidence for the view that efforts to coordinate macroeconomic policies are undesirable.

Constructive adjustments to, and reinterpretations of, the FR analysis emerged from the criticisms of Holtham and Hughes Hallett (HHH), first made in 1986 in response to the original FR paper and eventually published in full together with a response by FR.[12] HHH distinguish between "weak-condition" and "strong-condition" bargains in policy coordination. For a weak-condition bargain to be struck, each individual government must expect to gain according to its own preferred model, but each government does not ask whether the models preferred by other governments also predict that the individual government will gain. For a strong-condition bargain to be struck, each government must expect to gain not only according to its own model but also according to the preferred models of other governments. (HHH also discuss a "superstrong" bargain in which each government would expect to gain according to all available models.) HHH initially conjectured, and confirmed using FR's own calculations, that restricting coordination to instances in which a proposed package of policy changes satisfies a robustness criterion has the effect of significantly raising the frequency of outcomes that improve welfare.[13] For example, if the initial FR exercise is restricted

12. See Holtham and Hughes Hallett (1987), published in full in (1992); and Frankel, Erwin, and Rockett (1992).

13. Frankel and Rockett further confirmed the conclusion of Holtham and Hughes Hallett in a subsequent review of the original calculations. Frankel, Erwin, and Rockett (1992). Kenen (1989, p. 38) offers a double rationale for the Holtham and Hughes Hallett strong bargain: *prudence* requires a policymaker to ask whether his own economy would gain if the model of the other country's policymaker were true, while *reputation* requires him to ask whether the other country would gain if his model were true and he persuaded the other country's policymaker to take advice based on his model.

to strong-condition bargains (each government expects to gain according to its own and the other government's model), only 410 cases out of 1,000 result in actual coordination; within that subset, however, both the United States and the ROECD gain in slightly more than three-fourths of the cases. More generally, as the robustness requirement is tightened (that is, as both governments must expect to gain according to each of a larger proportion of the ten models), the number of cases of actual coordination shrinks further, but the probability of welfare gains rises still higher.[14]

Specific disagreement among national policymakers about competing models, notwithstanding the title of the original FR paper, seems less of a problem than the inability of any of the policymakers to know which model is least incorrect. HHH emphasize that when substantially differing views about models are present, acknowledgment of this situation can catalyze policymakers to focus on the robustness of conclusions stemming from the different models.[15] Of course, if competing models are greatly at odds and model uncertainty is severe, it may be impossible for policymakers from different nations to identify a robust, strong-condition bargain, and coordination will not occur.

Rex Ghosh and Paul Masson, in a series of important papers culminating in a 1994 book, have taken different tacks from FR and HHH in studying the implications of model uncertainty for international cooperation.[16] In a theoretical model drawn from a paper by Gilles Oudiz and Jeffrey Sachs, Ghosh showed that sufficiently high degrees of uncertainty could eliminate gains from coordination.[17] In a further theoretical exploration that partly reverses the earlier Ghosh result, however, Ghosh and Masson and Ghosh and Swati Ghosh derive conditions under which uncertainty, rather than precluding coordination, may provide an additional incentive to coordinate.[18] Ghosh and Masson emphasize learning issues and allow decisionmakers to update their priors in a Bayesian fashion over the set of possible models. Masson studies uncertainty about portfolio preferences and its interaction with the potential gains from coordination.[19] These

14. Frankel and Rockett (1992, table 1).
15. Holtham and Hughes Hallett (1992).
16. Ghosh and Masson (1994).
17. Oudiz and Sachs (1985); and Ghosh (1986).
18. Ghosh and Masson (1988); and Ghosh and Ghosh (1991).
19. Ghosh and Masson (1991); and Masson (1992).

various contributions are summarized and extended in the 1994 book.

Ghosh and Masson (hereafter GM) stress the distinction between "additive uncertainty" and "multiplier uncertainty."[20] They point out that the latter is much more important than the former for the gains from international coordination. Additive uncertainty does not change the ex ante, expected values of the policy spillovers from one nation to another (though it typically will affect the ex post, actual gains). Multiplier uncertainty, in contrast, does alter those cross-border spillovers and can significantly alter the expected as well as actual gains from coordination. Multiplier uncertainty can thus provide incentives to coordinate policies even when such incentives would not otherwise exist. GM also differentiate between "domestic" multiplier uncertainty and multiplier uncertainty associated with cross-border transmission of policy actions. They show that "a sufficiently high degree of uncertainty about domestic multipliers reduces the gains from coordination while increased transmission multiplier uncertainty raises the welfare gains."[21]

GM provide a model-based exposition of the point that increases in the magnitude of cross-border spillovers can magnify externalities and international collective-goods problems. They illustrate how changes in structural parameters for cross-border spillovers can alter the means and increase the variances of reduced-form transmission multipliers by much more than they affect the means and variances of reduced-form domestic multipliers.

Two more conclusions of GM warrant emphasis. Their analysis reinforces the point that national economies can become dynamically unstable and suffer welfare losses from efforts at coordination if policymakers assign little weight to the "correct" model and exhibit no learning behavior.[22] Under such circumstances, the performance of the GM model economies can be more robust under simple presumptive guidelines than with activist coordination. If policymakers can engage in Bayesian learning, however, the risks of dynamic instability are reduced, and the ex post gains from international policy coordination are systematically positive in the GM simulations.

20. The distinction originated with Brainard (1967).
21. Ghosh and Masson (1994, chap. 3, p. 71).
22. Ghosh and Masson (1991; 1994, chap. 6).

GM are appropriately cautious about their learning results, preferring not to make general claims about the desirability of policy coordination in the presence of model uncertainty. "At the very least, however," they write, "all of our results suggest that countries would be no worse off by coordinating their macroeconomic policies so long as policymakers do not stick dogmatically to incorrect models."[23]

The various points about model uncertainty made in this chapter lead to the conclusion that the *feasibility* of cooperation and coordination, not their desirability, should be the primary focus of attention in policy analysis. There is no question whatever that model uncertainty makes activist coordination very difficult, if not completely infeasible. Model uncertainty also makes it more difficult to agree on international cooperation through presumptive guidelines for rule-based national operating regimes.[24]

An extended target-zone proposal, to take only one prominent illustration, would require an internationally agreed calculation of the exchange rate zones. With some analytical procedures, such calculations would in turn entail understandings about appropriate and sustainable current account imbalances. Despite the work of John Williamson and others on "fundamental equilibrium exchange rates" (FEERs), difficult analytical questions remain unresolved about how to make such calculations merely in the context of a single multi-country model. The difficulties are made much greater by the competing-model problem. The available evidence, moreover, suggests that the performance of national economies in a target-zone international regime could depend quite sensitively on the choice of the FEERs.[25]

The posture that Holtham and Hughes Hallett recommend at the end of their comment on Frankel and Rockett's work appeals to me as a balanced assessment of the implications of model uncertainty for

23. Ghosh and Masson (1994, p. 166).

24. Ghosh and Masson reach a similar general conclusion: "Uncertainty, though making coordination more desirable, probably makes it more difficult to achieve and to sustain" (1994, p. 240).

25. Williamson (1991, 1993). For discussion, see Edison, Miller, and Williamson (1987); Hughes Hallett (1989, 1992, 1993); Hughes Hallett, Holtham, and Hutson (1989); Currie, Holtham, and Hughes Hallett (1989); and Currie and Wren-Lewis (1989a, 1989b, 1990). See also Williamson (1994). Williamson and Henning (1994), read in conjunction with the comments by Richard Cooper, Shijuro Ogata, and Niels Thygesen, give the flavor of the policy debate as of 1994.

the efforts of national governments to cooperate with one another. HHH argue that policymakers considering cooperation should "seek to use all available information to take account of uncertainty" but should not try to "suppress or eliminate any remaining differences in view." They should try to identify policies that promise gains on any of the views held by the participating countries. "There is no assurance that such policies exist in any particular case; but that is no reason not to look for them, nor to eschew bargains should such policies be found."[26]

The nuance that HHH do not emphasize enough is the importance of analytical backup for efforts to identify policies that promise gains. Ongoing consultations and information sharing can have great analytical value in reducing uncertainty about initial conditions and current shocks, and sometimes also about the current objectives and policy intentions of the decisionmakers participating in intergovernmental consultations. No less important, consultations and information exchanges *about competing models* can be analytically helpful because of their potential for reducing model uncertainty. International consultations designed to exchange information about alternative analytical models of the world economy seem to me an unambiguously helpful activity for the advisory staffs of policymakers. Indeed, I would go further: an improved analytical understanding of macroeconomic interactions among national economies is a prerequisite for making progress on virtually every significant macroeconomic issue, positive or normative, confronting national policymakers. This improved understanding is unquestionably required for more successful international cooperation about national stabilization policies.

26. Holtham and Hughes Hallet (1992, p. 1051).

Chapter 8

Cross-Border Spillovers: Major Features and Empirical Evidence

*T*HIS CHAPTER turns to the main features and transmission channels of cross-border spillovers among national economies. Focusing attention in this way complements the earlier, more abstract analysis of intergovernmental cooperation. The chapter concentrates on spillovers resulting from policy actions rather than those from nonpolicy disturbances. But all types of spillovers can have adverse consequences for receiving countries. And all types might trigger intergovernmental consultations about possible cooperation.

Major Features of Cross-Border Spillovers

For simplicity of exposition, imagine a world composed of only two hypothetical nations. Assume that one of the nations, labeled here as US, is like the United States in real life. Assume that the other nation, ROECD, is like an aggregate of the rest of the industrial countries in the Organization for Economic Cooperation and Development. The currency of the US will be referred to as the dollar, that of the ROECD as the ecu. Many of the important features of cross-border spillovers in real life can be simply described in this two-economy, one-exchange-rate context where complications from multiple nations and developing countries are suppressed.

I first summarize the probable consequences of a contractionary fiscal action adopted by US policymakers. As a second example, I consider an expansionary change in US monetary policy. Analogous consequences (with obvious changes in country or in sign) would be projected if ROECD rather than US policymakers were assumed to initiate comparable policy actions. For each policy action, the summary begins with own-country effects in the US, proceeds to the effects on the exchange rate and current account balances, and then focuses on the cross-border spillovers influencing the ROECD. All effects are discussed as deviations from a benchmark, "baseline" evolution of the two economies.[1]

US Fiscal Contraction. Suppose the US government announces a large, permanent decrease in real US government expenditures accompanied by a permanently decreased target ratio of US government debt to US nominal GDP.[2] As ancillary assumptions, suppose that (1) private sector agents in the US and the ROECD, and the ROECD government and central bank, do not expect any US fiscal action prior to this announcement; (2) the central bank in the US varies the US short-term interest rate so as to keep the US money stock close to its baseline target path ("unchanged" monetary policy thus being defined as no deviations of money from baseline); (3) the ROECD central bank similarly prevents the ROECD money stock from deviating significantly from its baseline path;[3] (4) the ROECD fiscal authority has a reaction function that varies ROECD taxation so as to keep the ratio of ROECD government debt to ROECD nominal GDP close to its baseline path; and (5) the exchange rate between the two economies fluctuates freely.

In the initial year, US output falls by somewhat more than the cut in government spending. The US price level and US interest rates also decline relative to baseline. During the second year and thereafter, "crowding-in" behavior is observed as the negative effects of the cut in government spending begin to be offset by increases in other spending on domestic output induced by lower interest rates, lower

1. The properties of the baseline are not germane here and therefore are left unspecified.

2. For example, the cut in expenditures might be measured as 2 percent of the baseline value of real US GDP (the constant-dollar amount growing gradually over time because of growth in baseline real GDP) and the target debt ratio might be lowered gradually over ten years relative to baseline by 15 basis points (say, from 0.55 to 0.40) and then maintained at that differential below baseline thereafter.

3. The "money-targeting" approach to monetary policy used here for illustration, assumed to be followed by both the US and ROECD central banks, is embodied in the reaction function of equation (1) in chapter 2, with the feedback parameter β having a fairly high value.

prices, and a depreciation of the dollar. Eventually—say, after four to six years—output will have moved upward most of the way back to its baseline path. Even in the medium run, US prices continue to decline further relative to baseline.

The direction of movement of the exchange value of a country's currency after a fiscal action is theoretically ambiguous. The direction depends on, most importantly, the degree of substitutability between assets denominated in the home currency and in foreign currencies.[4] In multicountry empirical models of recent vintage, the home currency typically depreciates in the initial years following a fiscal contraction.[5] In the example here, therefore, we can presume the US dollar depreciates in the short run. With the domestic economy softer and the dollar depreciating, the US current account balance improves relative to baseline. In the two-region context of this example, the improvement in the US current balance is associated with a mirror-image deterioration relative to baseline in the ROECD current account balance. And from the perspective of the ROECD, of course, the change in the exchange rate is seen as an appreciation of the ecu.

4. In simplified expositions of the theory, the direction of movement of the exchange rate depends on the relative slopes of the "BP" and "LM" curves (representing, respectively, equilibrium in the external sector and the money market). The greater the degree of substitutability between home-currency and foreign-currency assets, the flatter will be the slope of the BP curve. A flatter (steeper) slope for the BP curve than for the LM curve implies that a contractionary fiscal action will depreciate (appreciate) the home currency. In the textbook theoretical framework, the exchange rate responds to interest rates (via capital flows) and to income/absorption (via the effects through imports on the trade balance). A fiscal contraction tends to lower the home interest rate (putting pressure on the home currency to depreciate) and to reduce home income (putting pressure on the currency to appreciate by improving the trade balance). The flatter the BP curve relative to the LM curve, the more the interest-rate effects on the exchange rate dominate the effects working through income and the trade balance.

5. The empirical models tend to embody either perfect or near-perfect substitutability of assets denominated in different currencies (relatively flat BP curves). Exchange rates are determined for the most part in asset-market equations, for example via uncovered interest-parity conditions. Hence nominal exchange rates move in response to changes in nominal interest-rate differentials, expected inflation differentials, current and expected relative price levels (and, in a few cases, factors that may influence equilibrium real exchange rates in the long run such as the wealth of national residents and the stocks of governments' debts). In theoretical and empirical models, the home currency's exchange value often follows a complex dynamic pattern—for example, depreciating temporarily after a fiscal contraction but then eventually appreciating to an inflation-adjusted value significantly above its original level.

Changes in actual and expected exchange rates, in interest rates, and in the prices and volumes of cross-border trade are the primary channels through which the US fiscal action is transmitted to the ROECD. Suppose in the first instance that the ROECD authorities keep monetary and fiscal policy unchanged (in the senses defined earlier). In that case, real GDP in the ROECD falls (the unexpected US fiscal contraction is transmitted "positively" outside the US). The reductions in ROECD output lag behind those in the US and tend to be about one-fourth to one-third as large (measuring the deviations in the ROECD as a percentage of own GDP, as in the US). The ROECD price level falls, by growing amounts through time. Interest rates in the ROECD also fall relative to baseline, though less than in the US.

Consider now the dilemmas facing ROECD policymakers as a result of this unexpected US policy action. Given their expectations and preferences prior to the US action, and given their preferred resolution of the uncertainty and competing-model problems discussed in chapter 7, ROECD policymakers will probably have adjusted their policy instruments to achieve the best feasible outcome for ROECD ultimate-target variables they thought to be attainable. Now, however, they find that the US action will have bumped their target variables away from the preferred paths earlier identified. ROECD policymakers will thus now have an incentive to readjust the settings on ROECD policy instruments, trying to offset some or all of the unexpected consequences of the US policy action. Given the newly projected falls in output and inflation and the appreciation of the ecu stemming from the US fiscal contraction, ROECD policymakers may well wish to consider some sort of expansionary action with their monetary instruments, their fiscal instruments, or both.

One could make different assumptions about the situation confronting ROECD policymakers prior to the US action. For example, they could be assumed to be worried that ROECD aggregate demand would be undesirably strong but had felt constrained themselves from taking an assertive enough contractionary stance to offset that strength. Under such an assumption, ROECD policymakers might conceivably welcome the declines in output and inflation resulting from the US fiscal contraction. Conversely, ROECD policymakers might have initially believed that ROECD aggregate demand would already be too weak but had been hesitant to adopt an expansionary stance themselves sufficiently strong to offset that weakness. If that had been the expectation prior to the US action, ROECD policymakers would be particularly unhappy about the additional contractionary influences on the ROECD economy.

All things considered, however, the typical, most plausible assumption to make is that ROECD policymakers, prior to the unexpected US action, would have already done their best to judge the difficult trade-offs between goals such as inflation reduction and output growth. In the light of those judgments the policymakers would thus already have adjusted ROECD policy instruments, applying whatever expansionary or contractionary stimuli that seemed appropriate (given the entire range of forces they had been expecting that would influence the ROECD economy). The surprise US fiscal action, as judged by ROECD policymakers, will hence have adverse effects. The newly projected reduction in ROECD inflation stemming from the US fiscal contraction could conceivably be welcome considered in isolation. But the new fall in output will certainly be unwelcome. On balance, moreover, the newly projected combination of output and inflation following the US action will be judged inferior to the combination anticipated prior to the US action. The same point can be stated differently: if ROECD policymakers had been able to predict the US fiscal contraction, they would have chosen to be more expansionary with their own monetary policy or their own fiscal policy than they in fact initially chose to be.

US Monetary Expansion. Monetary-policy actions have qualitatively different consequences, but the cross-border spillovers resulting from them can likewise adversely buffet the decisions of foreign policymakers. To illustrate, suppose the US central bank announces that it intends to raise its target path for the US money stock above baseline in all future periods by a constant percentage amount, k. Assume as in the preceding example that the policy action is unexpected, that ROECD policy behavior is unchanged from baseline, and that the exchange rate fluctuates.[6]

The US monetary expansion initially causes a fall in US interest rates and increases in US output and the US price level (all relative to

---

6. US fiscal policy in this example is assumed to be unchanged in the sense that the US fiscal authority varies US taxation so as to keep the ratio of US government debt to US nominal GDP close to its baseline path.

baseline). The immediate fall in interest rates is sharp. Thereafter interest rates gradually rise back toward their baseline values. After an initial modest rise in the first year, real GNP tends to rise somewhat further in the second year; it then begins a protracted falling back toward baseline in subsequent years. This subsequent return of real GNP toward baseline accords with the "long-run neutrality of money" assumption of many theoretical models. The US price level rises continually, increasing above baseline somewhat further in every successive year.

The US monetary expansion leads to a sharp initial depreciation of the dollar, perhaps half again as large as the k percent increase in the target path for the money stock. The "overshooting" of the exchange rate is then gradually corrected in subsequent periods as the dollar climbs back toward an expected long-run value about k percent below baseline.

Expository theoretical models cannot predict unambiguously the effects of a monetary expansion on current account balances. Higher incomes and output in the originating (home) country tend to pull in more imports; thus the income-absorption effects of the monetary expansion work to worsen the home trade and current account balances. In contrast, the expenditure-switching effects associated with the home-currency depreciation tend to improve the home trade and current account balances. Either effect could in principle dominate the other. In multicountry empirical models of recent vintage, the absolute size of the net effects, whatever the sign, is small.

The spillover effects from a US monetary expansion on ROECD output and prices are also best described as small in absolute magnitude. Some empirical models predict a modest fall relative to baseline in ROECD outputs and prices, which reminds one of the "beggar-thy-neighbor" result of monetary expansion in simplified theoretical models with high capital mobility and static expectations for the exchange rate. But other models suggest small positive effects, which can arise in general theoretical models. Averaged across a variety of models, the shorter-run and medium-run effects are slightly negative. Interest rates in the ROECD fall slightly below baseline, but by a markedly smaller amount than in the US.

How will ROECD policymakers perceive the consequences of the surprise US monetary expansion? Several of their most important ultimate-target variables, notably ROECD real output and ROECD inflation, will not be expected to change greatly as a result of the US action; unlike fiscal-policy spillovers, monetary-policy spillovers have much smaller net effects on those variables. But the consequences of the US monetary action for other key ROECD variables are more significant. The appreciation of the ecu—which rises sharply relative to the earlier anticipated baseline after the announcement of the US action—is a key example. The perceived difficulties for ROECD policymakers could be especially great if they had specified a target zone for the exchange rate. But even if both countries are agreed on permitting flexibility in the exchange rate, the repercussions of the ecu appreciation inside the ROECD, political as well as economic, will be too large to ignore.

For the same types of reason discussed above for the spillovers of the US fiscal action, the ROECD policymakers will typically judge the consequences of the US monetary action to be adverse for the ROECD economy. Prior to the US action, ROECD policymakers will have done their best to make appropriate adjustments for ROECD policy instruments. Had they been able to predict the US monetary expansion in advance, they would have chosen marginally different instrument settings than those they did in fact select. The differences between initial instrument settings and the settings judged appropriate after learning of the US action tend to be smaller for monetary spillovers than fiscal spillovers. But even for monetary spillovers these differences are nonnegligible.

Empirical Evidence on the Importance of Spillovers and Externalities

For ease of exposition, the preceding section uses a hypothetical, two-nation framework. But the preceding judgments about the own-country and cross-border spillover effects of policy actions are grounded on the least inadequate empirical evidence available about real-life policy actions initiated by the United States and how such actions affect the economies of the rest of the Organization for Economic Cooperation and Development (OECD) in the aggregate.

Most of the existing empirical evidence stems from the efforts of a worldwide network of researchers who have been collaborating since the mid-1980s to improve knowledge about the interdependence of national economies. A fundamental premise has driven this research: before progress can be made on the positive and normative issues of macroeconomic policy facing national governments, analytical understanding of macroeconomic interactions among national economies must first improve.[7]

The initial research effort yielded a two-volume publication completed in 1987. Follow-up workshops and conferences focused on the U.S. current account balance, on Japanese-U.S. macroeconomic interactions, and on the behavior of financial sectors in interdependent economies. Linkages between the OECD and non-OECD economies were studied at a conference held in Korea in 1991. Another substantial installment of the continuing research effort, evaluating rule-based national operating regimes for monetary policy, was published in 1993.[8]

The empirical evidence generated by the research to date, as stressed in chapter 7, is subject to substantial uncertainty. Different models produce quantitatively different estimates, and the generalizations in this chapter about the spillover consequences of US policy actions are thus subject to revision in future research. At the very least, estimates of spillover effects must be treated as having wide

7. The organizing initiative for the series of projects was taken by a group of researchers sponsored by the Brookings Institution, with subsequent organizing support from a variety of other institutions, in particular the staffs of the Federal Reserve Board and the Japanese Economic Planning Agency and the Centre for Economic Policy Research in London. Support for the research was provided by, among others, the Ford Foundation, the Tokyo Club Foundation for Global Studies, and the MacArthur Foundation.

8. The initial 1987 volumes were published as Bryant and others, eds., *Empirical Macroeconomics for Interdependent Economies* (Brookings, 1988; referred to here as *EMIE*). Holtham (1986) is an early exposition of the data published in *EMIE*. The empirical evidence used by Fischer (1988) in his survey paper is from Holtham (1986). See also Frankel (1988a). Bryant, Holtham, and Hooper (1988) report the research on the U.S. current account balance. See Helliwell (1988), in the symposium sponsored by the Japanese Economic Planning Agency, on Japanese-U.S. macroeconomic interactions. Hooper and others (1990), the volume from the conference sponsored by the Federal Reserve Board, presents the research on financial-sector behavior in interdependent economies; see especially Helliwell, Cockerline, and Lafrance (1988). Bryant, Helliwell, and Hooper (1989) summarize the main empirical results of the research effort as of 1989 and as seen from a U.S. perspective. The Korea conference was jointly sponsored by the OECD, the Korea Development Institute, the Brookings Institution, and the Centre for Economic Policy Research; Bryant and McKibbin (1994) analyze the empirical simulations prepared for that conference. The monetary-regime analysis is in Bryant, Hooper, and Mann, *Evaluating Policy Regimes* (1993). See also Ghosh and Masson (1994) for empirical evidence on cross-border spillovers.

confidence intervals around the estimated means.[9] Remember also, of course, that the cross-border spillover effects of policy actions and nonpolicy disturbances obviously vary with the size of the actions, with the relative importance and relative openness of the originating country in the world economy, and with alternative assumptions made about the domestic operating regimes used by countries for their monetary policies and their fiscal policies.

The Potential for Cooperation: An Illustrative Episode

As explained by the examples about the consequences of US fiscal and monetary actions for the ROECD, the usual situation confronting national policymakers is that unexpected economic developments originating abroad will be unwelcome. Such spillovers create additional uncertainty. They typically have effects on the home economy judged to be adverse. The more skillful are national policymakers in selecting settings for their instruments, the more unwelcome will be new policy or nonpolicy shocks originating outside the nation.

Because unexpected shocks emanating from policy actions taken abroad typically have adverse consequences for home-country macroeconomic management, a potential will exist for intergovernmental cooperation. To apply the analysis in earlier chapters to the examples here: if the ROECD and US governments can jointly take into account the spillovers of US actions into the ROECD, each government has the potential for using its policy instruments more effectively and thereby to attain higher levels of national welfare. Of course, policy coordination does not eliminate the difficult trade-offs between competing national objectives facing both the ROECD and the US. Nor can policy coordination eliminate difficult trade-offs among the countries to the extent that they seek partially conflicting goals. But policy coordination can, in principle, enable policymakers to manage the difficult trade-offs better than they otherwise could.

An illustrative episode, drawn from the latter part of the 1980s, helps to give concreteness to the general points above. I deliberately choose an episode that did *not* give rise to successful cooperation. This

9. Bryant, Helliwell, and Hooper (1989) provide rough indications of the width of confidence intervals around estimates averaged across different models.

choice illustrates the potential for mutual gains and the obstacles that often inhibit the gains from being realized.

In 1987 growth in real output for the world economy as a whole was disappointingly sluggish, while inflation rates were modest (and much lower than earlier in the 1980s). Fears of a resumption of inflation, however, were widespread and strong. Current account imbalances among the major industrial countries remained very large; the U.S. external deficit was still running at an annual rate of some $150 billion to $160 billion, and the combined external surpluses of Japan, Germany, and a few other European countries added up to a comparably large figure. The disappointingly sluggish growth in output expected for the industrial countries combined with disappointingly slow progress in reducing current account imbalances caused most analysts to form a relatively bearish outlook for the world economy as a whole (and in particular for developing countries).

Given these circumstances, what changes in the macroeconomic policies of the industrial countries could have significantly improved the outlook?[10] The burgeoning structural deficit in the budget of the U.S. federal government was widely regarded as a major cause of the growing domestic and external imbalances afflicting the U.S. economy. Analysts thus frequently espoused contractionary fiscal action for the United States.

Contractionary U.S. fiscal action, if sufficiently large, could have substantially reduced the U.S. budget deficit. And, as explained above, interest rates would have fallen, in the United States and abroad, and the U.S. dollar would have depreciated relative to ROECD currencies. Price levels would have fallen below the paths that would otherwise have prevailed in the United States and ROECD economies. The consequences for price levels would have been welcomed. But U.S. real GNP and employment would have fallen well below the paths they otherwise would have followed. And ROECD output and employment would likewise have been reduced, by perhaps one-fourth to one-third of the percentage decline in the

10. In my discussion of this historical period, I do not discuss intervention in the exchange markets, and in particular do not highlight the Plaza Accord of September 1985 and the Louvre Accord of February 1987. In my view, the exchange rate aspects of these accords are less consequential than the domestic policies I emphasize in the text. See Funabashi (1988) for a narrative account of this historical period focusing on exchange rates and exchange-market intervention.

United States. Given the already sluggish performance of economic activity in the OECD economies, this additional downward pressure on output and employment would have been quite discomforting to ROECD governments. Such softness in world aggregate demand would also have been damaging to the prospects for export receipts and growth in the economies of developing countries.

Suppose that the Federal Reserve in the United States had adopted a more expansionary monetary policy in conjunction with the fiscal contraction. If such a monetary expansion had been pronounced, it could even have offset a major part of the dampening effects on U.S. real GNP of the fiscal contraction (after, however, an initial transition period in which the fiscal contraction had stronger effects than the monetary expansion). The resulting reduction in the U.S. external deficit and in the external surpluses of ROECD countries might have been no less substantial than from the U.S. fiscal contraction alone. (A U.S. monetary expansion alone, as already noted, reduces U.S. interest rates relative to ROECD interest rates and depreciates the dollar but tends not to change current account balances in either direction by a large amount.) Inflation in the United States and in ROECD countries might not have differed greatly from the inflation rates that would otherwise have prevailed. Roughly speaking, the upward pressure on the U.S. price level associated with the U.S. monetary expansion would have been countered by the downward pressure from the fiscal contraction. In the ROECD countries, inflation rates would tend to have been reduced by the U.S. fiscal contraction and by the U.S. monetary expansion; both actions would have caused an appreciation of the ROECD currencies. The combined U.S. policy actions, however, would still have generated adverse consequences for real economic activity outside the United States. The hypothesized shift in the mix of U.S. fiscal and monetary policies, just as with a U.S. fiscal contraction alone, would have caused a sizable reduction in real incomes and output in ROECD countries in the absence of adjustment in ROECD governments' policies.

As a further set of hypothesized policy modifications, therefore, imagine international consultations among the U.S. government and major ROECD governments that would have produced a cooperatively designed package of policy actions. Imagine that the United States had adopted fiscal contractionary measures and an offsetting expansion of monetary policy, but perhaps both being somewhat more modest in size than if the United States had decided to act in isolation. Concurrently, imagine that Japan, Germany, and several other European countries had expanded domestic demand to offset the decline in external demand associated with the change in U.S. policies. The ROECD expansionary actions might have been monetary, fiscal, or a modest mixture of each.

This hypothetical combination of policy modifications would have yielded a substantial improvement in the output performances of all OECD countries. Price levels in ROECD countries, to be sure, could have been marginally higher than without any of the policy changes. Given the initial conditions of 1987–88, however, there would have been minimal risks of a worldwide resumption of inflationary conditions. Current account imbalances among the OECD economies would have been sharply reduced. The predicted consequences for real incomes and output, inflation rates, and current account imbalances vary somewhat according to whether the ROECD expansionary actions are hypothesized to be monetary or fiscal. And judgments about how large the net, overall improvement in economic welfare would have been—for individual countries or for the world economy as a whole—depend, of course, on the relative weights assigned to output gains and reductions in current account imbalances versus changes in price levels. Nevertheless, unless macroeconomic performance is judged almost exclusively in terms of inflation, the hypothesized combination of policy changes could have greatly improved the world economic outlook.

In sum, the potential for mutual gains through activist coordination of macroeconomic policies was substantial. In principle, both the United States and ROECD countries could have benefited. The essence of the cooperative agreement would have required the U.S. government to credibly bring its budget under better control and to adjust its monetary policy in an accommodating way while ROECD governments credibly acted to expand domestic demand to prevent their economies from growing too sluggishly or falling into recession. A jointly agreed statement of goals and the policies to foster the goals could have supported each country's individual actions. The intergovernmental cooperation could have created a climate of improved confidence, and of stability in expectations, helpful in preventing either recession or a resumption of rapid inflation.

The coordinated package of policy modifications sketched here was not adopted in 1987–88. The possibility of such an international bargain may have been bruited in a few intergovernmental discussions, but essentially the idea never came off the drawing board.

Part of the explanation for this situation can be attributed to analytical uncertainty. The economic analysis summarized above did not command consensus among OECD governments. Some ROECD governments were reluctant to stimulate aggregate demand because they believed, in contrast to most of the available evidence, that expansionary policy actions taken by them would be ineffective in raising output. Others believed that stimulation of demand would be excessively inflationary. Governmental understanding of cross-border spillover effects was limited. The model uncertainty stressed in chapter 7 was too great for policymakers to believe that international coordination would be desirable.

As has often been the case with potential international coordination of macroeconomic policies, however, another important set of obstacles was political. The different parts of the potential international bargain in 1987–88 could not stand on their own. An agreement could only have been designed and implemented if each major government could have been counted on to deliver its contribution. If a major government was suspected of not being willing to play or of having to withdraw one of its potential cards, the entire agreement, no matter how sensible its economics, would prove to be a house of cards.

Understandably, ROECD governments were especially reluctant to stimulate domestic demand in their economies without credible assurance that the United States would bring its structural budget deficit under better control. The governments of Germany and Japan, for example, would certainly not have participated in internationally agreed actions whose global consequences they considered inflationary. A boost to ROECD demand with an out-of-control U.S. budget—hence the possibility of excessive domestic demand in the United States—could have risked the resumption of worldwide inflation. A shift in the composition of world aggregate demand, reducing domestic demand in the United States and raising it in ROECD economies, would have been much more likely to command acceptance than an increase in total world demand.

Unfortunately, the U.S. government was in no position to give credible assurances about its ability to deliver a U.S. fiscal contraction, even if ROECD governments could give credible assurances of their ability to sustain expansionary actions. Domestic political debate within the United States was characterized by general lip service to the desirability of reducing the budget deficit and deadlock about the methods for doing so. The U.S. administration blamed Congress for inaction; Congress blamed the administration; stalemate dragged on. A domestic political compromise was not possible without including some form of tax increases in a budget package alongside cuts in government expenditures. Political support for tax increases could not be mobilized.[11]

In the absence of more auspicious domestic political conditions, especially in the United States but also within several other OECD countries, the potential for economic gains from international coordination in the late 1980s could not be realized. The existence of likely potential gains from intergovernmental cooperation is obviously a necessary, but is just as obviously not a sufficient, condition for cooperation to occur in practice.

11. The political deadlock persisted into the early 1990s. The structural budget deficit continued to worsen until August 1993, when the U.S. Congress and administration enacted a package of deficit reductions (including both expenditure cuts and tax increases) and reforms in the budget process in the Omnibus Budget Reconciliation Act of 1993.

Chapter 9

Evolution of National Policies and International Institutions

CHAPTERS 2 through 7 concentrated on analytical points rather than actual experience. Chapter 8 began a discussion that illustrates how the analysis can be applied to historical episodes. I now turn to further observations about real-life manifestations of intergovernmental consultations and cooperation, in particular the institutional contexts in which they have occurred. I begin with generalizations about historical experience. I conclude with normative recommendations for facilitating progress over the medium and longer runs.

Historical Experience

In the 1990s a variety of institutional forums exist for international (as opposed to merely regional) consultations about macroeconomic policies. The most prominent are the annual summit meetings of G-7 heads of state and the periodic meetings of G-7 finance ministers and central bank governors, supplemented by contacts and meetings among the G-7 sherpas or finance ministry deputies. Other influential forums include the regular meetings of central bank governors at the Bank for International Settlements; the periodic meetings of the Interim Committee of the International Monetary Fund (IMF), backed up by regular meetings of the IMF Executive Board; and meetings of ministers and of the Economic Policy Committee and its Working Parties (especially Working Party 3) at the OECD. These forums are ongoing activities. If a perceived crisis with implications for macroeconomic policies arises, the forums are sometimes also called into play for discussion and management of the crisis.

During the decades since World War II, intergovernmental consultations and cooperation about macroeconomic policies have been episodic. Periods characterized by considerable, sometimes even intense, activity have alternated with times in which efforts flagged noticeably. Several of the episodes of greatest activity have been initiated by periods of crisis (see chapter 5). The effective performance and the prestige of the institutional forums have tended to fluctuate up and down with the episodic cooperative efforts.

The early postwar years witnessed a flurry of activity, including the successful conclusion of top-level negotiations establishing the Bretton Woods institutions (the IMF and the World Bank) and the General Agreement on Tariffs and Trade (GATT). The Marshall Plan contributed to the rebuilding of Europe. This period in some respects was a high-water mark for economic cooperation among the largest industrial nations. It was also a period, however, in which political and economic power was unusually asymmetric. If the theory of a hegemonic power inducing "hegemonic stability" has empirical validity, the dominant position of the United States in the early postwar years probably provides the strongest evidence.

The United States did not permit the IMF to be an effective central forum for cooperation in the 1950s. European governments, led by France, began to challenge the dominance of U.S. views on international monetary issues in the 1960s. Nonetheless, the Bretton Woods era in the 1950s and 1960s maintained a fairly high degree of intergovernmental consultation. Working Party 3 of the OECD functioned quite effectively as a key forum for these discussions. The creation of special drawing rights (SDRs) in the second half of the 1960s is a noteworthy illustration of successful international macroeconomic cooperation.[1]

By the end of the 1960s, an increasingly integrated world economy and linked financial markets were experiencing greater cross-border pressures; intergovernmental tensions about economic matters were growing. The breakdown of the Bretton Woods exchange rate ar-

1. For the top-level negotiations and the immediate postwar period, see Gardner (1969). Solomon (1982) provides a perspective on the Bretton Woods era as a whole. Horsefield (1969) and de Vries (1976) provide more detail, including essential documents, about the IMF.

rangements in 1971–73 and the first major increase by OPEC countries in their oil prices in 1973–74 severely strained the international
institutions and the political impulses to cooperation. In response to
these turbulent events, to be sure, a sustained effort was made to
reconfigure the international regime environment (to "reform the
international monetary system") through the negotiations of the
Committee of Twenty. But in the end, only a minimalist rewriting of
the IMF Articles of Agreement proved possible.[2]

The 1973–74 increases in oil prices gave rise to extensive intergovernmental discussions designed to preclude mutually defeating efforts to avoid surges in current account deficits or competitive
currency appreciations. Special oil-adjustment facilities were created
within the IMF. An International Energy Agency was established.
With the wisdom of hindsight, we now know that the supply shock
aspects of the increases in oil prices were not well understood at the
time. Some aspects of macroeconomic policies were designed less
than satisfactorily. Not all the cooperative understandings embodied
in the International Energy Agency may have been wise. Even so,
extensive international consultations focused on the problems. It was
well recognized, and acknowledged in intergovernmental communi-
ques, that decentralized national policies could have systemic effects
that were counterproductive. I personally doubt that international
cooperation focused on the oil price increases itself created adverse
consequences. My inclination is to judge international cooperation in
that period as modestly successful on balance.

The annual economic summit meetings, initially including only the
five largest industrial countries (G-5) but subsequently expanded to
the seven largest (G-7), were initiated at Rambouillet in 1975. The
1977 London and 1978 Bonn summits, sometimes praised and even
more often criticized, were the most ambitious of postwar efforts to
actually *coordinate* economic policies. The second major increase in
world oil prices, catalyzed by revolutionary developments and the fall
of the shah in Iran, followed shortly after the 1978 summit. That
dramatic, unforeseen change in world economic conditions, which is
not always analyzed correctly and put into appropriate perspective in
descriptions of that period, accounts for much of the contentious
appraisal of the Bonn 1978 summit agreement. In my view, the

2. Solomon (1982); Williamson (1977); de Vries (1976); and Fischer (1988).

1977–78 economic summit consultations are examples of modestly successful international economic cooperation.[3]

Subsequent years were characterized by continued economic turbulence. With the election of Ronald Reagan as U.S. president, a significant change in economic ideology occurred in the United States in the early 1980s—including attitudes about the benefits and costs of international cooperation. The early 1980s thus witnessed an ebbing of commitment to international discussions and cooperation, especially to consideration of the coordination of national macroeconomic policies.

By 1985 dissatisfaction with the experience of the early 1980s was high. The U.S. dollar had appreciated against other major currencies by large amounts, and even the U.S. government (helped greatly by the appointment in early 1985 of a differently minded treasury secretary) had reached the conclusion that cooperative efforts to intervene in exchange markets could be beneficial. The latter half of the 1980s thus was a time when international consultations and cooperation were again more in favor. Unlike at the Plaza Hotel meeting in September 1985, however, at which all the governments agreed on concerted intervention that would be appropriate, the postures of the governments were frequently in conflict. Proposals for "coordination," as often in the past, were little more than hopes that *other* nations would take policy actions that would prove beneficial for the proposing nation.

Cooperation in October 1987 represents another example of successful intergovernmental consultations and coordinated crisis management. Many national stock markets fell sharply together in a period of a few days during that month. A coordinated, temporary easing of monetary policies (an expansion of liquidity that was subsequently reversed after confidence returned) in several of the G-7 countries helped to assuage worries that the market crashes would persist. Concerns that any one central bank might have had that its own currency would depreciate unduly in response to a unilateral lowering of its interest rates were dissipated when the central banks promptly acted together.

In the early years of the 1990s, the world economy was buffeted by further disruptions of global consequence—for example, the Persian

---

3. Putnam and Bayne (1984, chap. 6); Putnam and Henning (1989); and Holtham (1989a) analyze the 1977–78 summit meetings in detail.

Gulf War, reunification of West and East Germany, the collapse of the Soviet Union, and the associated turbulence in eastern Europe. These events constituted renewed stimuli for international cooperation but also posed new substantive and institutional difficulties.[4]

Generalizations from Historical Experience

My perspective on the episodic postwar experience with international macroeconomic cooperation leads me to several generalizations. As with all generalizations, exceptions and details have to be suppressed.

First, recent history has been characterized by substantial variation in the types and intensities of shocks hitting the global economy and individual national economies. During periods in which shocks have been large and created major changes in macroeconomic conditions, government officials have been confronted with augmented uncertainty about appropriate adjustments in their stabilization policies. The net implications of the augmented uncertainty for intergovernmental cooperation are ambiguous. Uncertainty in general makes cooperation more difficult (chapter 7). Yet if the shocks have pronounced cross-border consequences and seem to threaten crisis conditions, governments also have sharply increased incentives to try to manage the crisis (chapter 5).

Some periods have certainly been characterized by a crisis atmosphere and have triggered intergovernmental efforts to manage the crises. Variations in underlying shocks and economic conditions have thus been an important factor explaining the episodic nature of governments' efforts to consult and cooperate. Unexpected large shocks occurring after particular coordinating actions have been implemented have also been a major reason why the international coordination of macroeconomic policies is a contentious subject for debate.[5]

---

4. For discussion of developments in the later 1970s and the 1980s, see among others Horne and Masson (1988); Putnam and Bayne (1984); Fischer (1988, 1994); Artis and Ostry (1986, chap. 4); Dobson (1991); Solomon (1991, 1994); and Ghosh and Masson (1994).

5. The second oil shock following on the heels of the Bonn 1978 summit is the archetypal example.

Second, the postwar period has been characterized by up-and-down variation in the political inputs to international macroeconomic cooperation. These fluctuations—in political awareness of the potential benefits and in the willingness to exert leadership to explore opportunities for cooperation—have been an additional factor explaining the episodic nature of cooperative activities. On the whole, I do not detect a discernible secular increase in the political willingness to cooperate. And most observers would assign the political factors a less important role than that owed to fluctuations in the nature and severity of underlying shocks.

From one perspective, it may seem surprising that the political propensity of national governments to cooperate has not gradually increased over recent decades.[6] The premise underlying this entire series of Integrating National Economies books, after all, is that many types of cross-border spillovers have gradually increased in intensity. In turn these increases in interdependence have reduced the effects of an individual nation's policy instruments on national variables relative to the effects on variables in other countries. With this diminution in the relative potency of national policies, it may seem natural to expect that governments would wish to cooperate to help offset the decreased autonomy of national policies. Whether this expectation is in fact natural, or whether instead one might infer that intergovernmental cooperation is less important because policy instruments are less effective, is a difficult unresolved issue that cannot be tackled carefully here.

My third generalization is that the episodic nature of international macroeconomic cooperation cannot be attributed, at least not in a major way, to unevenness in the pace of evolution of the international institutions and forums. Although the existing institutional forums could have been strengthened somewhat, the forums themselves do not seem to me to have been a major impediment to improved consultations or to more effective efforts to coordinate policies.

Fourth, the episodic ups and downs in international macroeconomic cooperation cannot be readily explained by changes over time in the basic analytical difficulties that inhibit cooperation. (Note that

---

6. Detecting a secular trend in the political propensity to cooperate is of course not straightforward. Empirical measures do not exist. My generalization rests on personal observation and reading over the past three decades.

I am distinguishing between institutional structures themselves, the subject of the preceding generalization, versus the analytical knowledge and resources available to them. Later in the chapter I discuss the two subjects together.) Owing to limited improvements in knowledge and modeling capabilities, the analytical difficulties were a bit less severe at the beginning of the 1990s than in the 1950s and 1960s. Modest progress was made in the macroeconomic analysis of domestic economies. Limited but not dramatic progress was made in the analysis of cross-border macroeconomic interactions (chapter 8). Even so, model uncertainty remained severe throughout all the postwar decades. The small improvements in analytical understanding of the global economy are not promising candidates for explaining why some eras witnessed greater cooperative activity than others.

The preceding generalizations refer broadly to the world economic system as a whole and worldwide cooperation. If one instead focuses only on macroeconomic cooperation within regions, the generalizations have to be amended. The picture looks especially different if one concentrates on western Europe alone. Like the global economy, regions have also experienced heterogeneous variation in the types and intensities of shocks. The basic analytical difficulties that inhibit macroeconomic cooperation are highly relevant within regions as well as among regions. But the episodic variation in *political* inputs to cooperation tend to be somewhat less pronounced within regions. The evolution of the European Community, now European Union, has been associated with a gradual, persistent increase in macroeconomic cooperation—much of it triggered by the constraints of the European Monetary System and desires for eventual European monetary union, but some of it attributable to other pressures from European regional integration. Moreover, consultative processes and institutions of the European Union have also been gradually strengthened.[7]

To add perspective, the four preceding generalizations about macroeconomic cooperation should also be seen in the light of developments in intergovernmental cooperation outside the area of macroeconomic policies. Analytical difficulties in certain regulatory or

7. For references about cross-border cooperation within Europe and the evolutionary adaptation of European regional institutions, see, for example, Wallace (1994); Eichengreen (1992, 1993, 1994); Kenen (1992); Giavazzi and Giovannini (1989); Sbragia (1992a); and Centre for Economic Policy Research (1993).

microeconomic areas, though notable, are often less an obstacle than for macroeconomic policies. Political impediments to cooperation are also sometimes less severe. Consider three examples. Problems associated with cross-border collective goods have become gradually more important in the area of the regulation and supervision of financial institutions. Quite substantial progress in dealing with these problems has occurred in the past two decades, illustrated by the Concordats on supervision of banks' foreign establishments and by the capital-adequacy guidelines developed by the Committee on Banking Regulations and Supervisory Practices at the Bank for International Settlements. Bank fraud and bank failures with cross-border spillovers, such as the notorious cases of Bank of Commerce and Credit International in 1991 and Baring Brothers in early 1995, appear to have been well handled by international cooperation among bank supervisory authorities.[8] Nascent cooperative efforts in the environmental area, such as the Montreal protocol to reduce emission of chlorofluorocarbons to mitigate stratospheric ozone depletion, have borne significant fruit. Despite the agenda of accumulating problems, progress on issues pertaining to natural resources and the environment has probably outpaced progress in international macroeconomic cooperation.[9] The microeconomic area of product standards, contentious though it is, has also witnessed significant developments in international cooperation.[10] The limited but noteworthy progress in these other areas cautions against holding a pessimistic view about the long-run prospects for international cooperation about macroeconomic stabilization policies.

Given the historical experience of the postwar decades and the preceding generalizations, should one conclude that international macroeconomic cooperation has been deficient, that too little effort has been put into international consultations and too little support given to international institutions? Or given the difficulties and the domestic political constraints, should one instead be surprised that so much effort has been put into cooperative activities and that international institutions play as prominent a role as they do? Both per-

8. See the Integrating National Economies book by Herring and Litan (1995) and the earlier account by Bryant (1987a, chap. 8) for discussion of international cooperation among bank regulatory and supervisory authorities.

9. See the INE book by Cooper (1994) for discussion of international cooperation on natural resources and the environment.

10. This area is reviewed in the INE book by Sykes (1995).

spectives have some validity, in my judgment, though the undramatic truth lies somewhere in between.

A verdict that macroeconomic cooperation has been deficient seems especially appropriate for a few periods, for example the early and mid-1980s, when political will flagged and the efforts of key governments to cooperate were unusually timid. In those episodes, the rhetoric in favor of enhanced cooperation, and much more so the substance, fell well short of what would probably have been feasible and desirable. Even in more auspicious periods, moreover, governments have had a propensity to be shortsighted. Typically, an individual government has favored consultations and coordination when, in effect, its own participation might induce favorable behavior by other governments, but not when the process would uncomfortably constrain its own options. Just as superstition is some other person's religion and protectionism is some other nation's commercial policy, stubborn attachment to outmoded ideas of national sovereignty inhibits *other* nations from participating in mutually beneficial efforts at international cooperation.

Nonetheless, the opposite verdict—that cooperation has been surprisingly vigorous—also contains important elements of truth. Much of political and institutionalist analysis, for example, reminds us of the domestic political structures and attitudes that constrain government officials from ambitious efforts to cooperate. All things considered, political leadership has sometimes been able to catalyze intergovernmental cooperation even when the odds would have led analysts to conclude it could not be done.

Between the two extreme verdicts, my own views are closer to the latter perspective than to the assertion that cooperation has been uniformly deficient. I would disagree sharply with an assertion that political timidity and shortsightedness have been the overriding impediments to international consultations and coordination. The lack of convergence in analytical views about how national economies interact with one another has often been an equally severe impediment.

As historical studies in other areas have shown—for example, Richard Cooper's analysis of international efforts during the nineteenth and early twentieth centuries to control the spread of contagious diseases, or Peter Haas's account of recent international agreements to ban chlorofluorocarbons to protect stratospheric ozone—governments are likely to forge an agreement for dealing with a problem only after they, or the "epistemic community" of relevant professional analysts, have reached consensus in diagnosing the problem and identifying measures that will alleviate it.[11] Consensus on an appropriate analytical framework, as well as on the objective to be pursued, is a necessary—though, again, not a sufficient—condition for successful international cooperation.[12]

Because of this last point, I reserve my harshest criticisms of the historical experience for the failure of governments to place greater emphasis on improving analytical knowledge about the functioning of the world economy. One can, it is true, point to some examples of government officials encouraging and catalyzing relevant research. OECD staff members in the 1960s and 1970s were encouraged to develop a capacity for systemic analysis of the world economy (though government support waned in the 1980s). Parts of the IMF staff in the 1980s became active in research that tried to model the world economy (though not with notable support from national governments). The Federal Reserve system in the United States continued a long tradition of supporting macroeconomic modeling. Examples can be found in several other central banks or government agencies. The study of official intervention in exchange markets resulting in the Jurgensen report and its associated staff papers is a rare illustration of background research sponsored collectively by governments.[13] By and large, however, research has not received priority attention from government officials.

Likely Evolution in the Short Run

How may cooperative efforts focused on macroeconomic policies proceed in the next few years? The best guess is that national governments will continue with roughly the same patterns of behavior they

11. Cooper (1989); and Haas (1992b).

12. Dobson (1994), when discussing reasons for "divergences between normative preconditions for successful coordination and realities of G-7 experience in the 1980s," emphasizes the same point: "We learned that we do not have very good analytical tools; not enough is known about how economies actually work and how policies are transmitted across borders. In the 1990s, continuing structural change has exacerbated this situation" (p. C-145). For definition of an epistemic community and the role of such communities in international relations, see P. Haas (1992a, 1992b; also 1990) and Sebenius (1992) .

13. Working Group on Exchange Market Intervention (1983).

followed in the first half of the 1990s. If and when new shocks or new crises occur, international consultations might be modestly enhanced and, possibly, some additional cooperative undertakings might be tried. But substantially increased attempts to foster an activist international coordination of policies among the large industrial countries seem unlikely, with the possible exception of strengthened regional attempts in the European Community.

The various existing institutions and forums do serve, and are perceived by national governments as serving, important communicative goals. They are the primary sites of intergovernmental consultations. Indeed, they constitute the core of the existing weak international regime environment for macroeconomic stabilization policies. I see little evidence that consultations and information exchanges through these forums became significantly more intense on average in the 1980s and so far in the 1990s. During times of perceived crisis, consultations became more intense, but that observations applies with equal force to the more distant past. Speaking loosely, the regime environment was firmly established but subject to few adaptations and enhancements. For the near-term future, in the absence of crisis situations this "business as usual" climate is likely to continue.

The existing procedures for international exchanges of forecasts and current economic information are an important subset of these consultations. Some of this activity occurs through the OECD and has an influence on the OECD staff's analysis in the *OECD Economic Outlook*. In recent years, as part of the G-7 consultation process and the preparation of the IMF's *World Economic Outlook,* the IMF staff has participated more actively in such consultations. The substantive content of the G-7 consultations has been marginally improved as a result of the IMF participation. Informally, with less detail, and without public release of the analysis, an analogous exchange of views among central banks takes place at the monthly meetings of the Bank for International Settlements. As discussed below, over the longer run this type of consultation procedure can be greatly improved. For the shorter run, it seems unlikely that major changes are feasible (because governments do not appear to want them).

Beginning in the latter part of the 1980s, consultations among the G-7 nations have deemphasized exchange-rate, monetary, and budgetary policies of the G-7 nations themselves and the possible cross-border coordination of these policies. Other subjects of mutual interest have increased in relative importance. Conditions in the former Soviet Union and Eastern Europe and possible financial and technical assistance from the G-7 nations to those regions have featured prominently. Collective measures to ease the debt crisis in developing countries occupied center stage in the 1980s. Other such topics have included trade policies (especially the Uruguay round of trade negotiations prior to their conclusion in 1994), energy and energy security issues, and "structural" reforms within domestic economies. For the near-term future, the tendency to concentrate on subjects other than macroeconomic policy coordination is likely to continue.[14]

The sharp depreciation of the Mexican peso after December 1994 and subsequent fears about defaults on Mexican government debt illustrate how a new crisis, especially one judged to have possible systemic implications, can catalyze reevaluation of existing procedures and institutions. In early 1995 the IMF established by far the largest standby lending arrangement in its history for Mexico. Precedents and normal presumptions about the amount that an individual nation can borrow from the IMF were set aside because the circumstances were deemed exceptional. Moreover, the G-7 consultations in spring 1995 cautiously considered possible new cooperative actions—for example, the creation of an international "emergency fund" to mitigate disruptive capital flows and some form of a special "work-out facility" to smooth government-debt problems of the types associated with the Mexican crisis. (At the time this book went to press in summer 1995, it seemed unlikely that any of the more ambitious new proposals would command general acceptance by the G-7 or the Interim Committee. Yet the Mexican crisis, combined with sharp appreciations in the early months of 1995 of the Japanese yen and European currencies against the U.S. dollar, had at a minimum reignited old concerns and caused some governments to marginally rethink their views on international macroeconomic cooperation.)

14. Observers who are skeptical about the usefulness of efforts to coordinate macroeconomic policies under any circumstances, for example, Polak (1981, 1991), tend to applaud the recent focus of international consultations on topics other than exchange-rate, monetary, and fiscal policies. Others with a less skeptical view, for example, Dobson (1993), Bergsten and Williamson (1994), and Goldstein (1995), regret the lesser emphasis. The evolution of macroeconomic consultations and coordination in a regional context, particularly within western Europe, is again a partial exception to the trend identified in the text; see Wallace (1994); Eichengreen (1992, 1993); and Eichengreen and Wyplosz (1993).

Desirable Changes for the Medium Run:
Enhanced Analytical Support

I have stressed that an improved analytical understanding of macroeconomic interactions among national economies is a prerequisite for the development of enhanced cooperation through presumptive guidelines for rule-based national operating regimes or for more successful efforts at activist coordination. When I formulate normative recommendations for the longer-run future, therefore, my primary emphasis is on ways that governments might more actively encourage the development of analytical support for their efforts to promote strengthened "multilateral surveillance."[15]

In the past, the governments of the major countries have taken little direct interest in promoting an improvement in analytical understanding. Nor have they put pressure on the international organizations to make this objective a high priority for staff work. Such efforts as have been made have been sponsored by individual central banks, or individual groups within international organizations, or research or academic institutions.

The paucity of analytical support for international consultations has been more pronounced than can be explained by the inadequacies of existing knowledge. The series of annual summits and G-7 ministers' meetings has had even less continuity and institutional infrastructure than consultations conducted through the IMF, the OECD, or the Bank for International Settlements. G-7 meetings have not been backstopped by consistent staff support. The G-7 governments have not wanted to establish a new secretariat to support the G-7 process and at the same time have been unwilling to allow existing international organizations such as the IMF or OECD to become actively enough involved to play that role.[16]

15. The phrase "multilateral surveillance" is the most often encountered term for cooperative systemic oversight of nations' macroeconomic policies. The term surveillance stems in part from Article IV, section 3 of the IMF's Articles of Agreement, which requires the Fund to "oversee the international monetary system in order to ensure its effective operation" and, to fulfill that function, to "exercise firm surveillance over the exchange rate policies of members." Because domestic macroeconomic policies are a fundamental determinant of exchange rates, effective surveillance requires consideration of the whole range of domestic macroeconomic policies.

16. The extent to which the managing director and staff of the IMF are involved in preparatory analysis for G-7 meetings, and in the meetings themselves, is discussed in Crockett (1989, pp. 359–60); Solomon (1991, pp. 110–11); Dobson (1991, p. 32; 1994, p. 146); Fischer (1994, pp. C161–62); and Goldstein (1995, pp. 32–34).

This aspect of international economic cooperation is also unlikely to change in the short run. But it could—and should—be strengthened over the medium and long runs. Several years ago, I sketched a vision of how the institutional evolution of international macroeconomic cooperation might proceed.[17] In that sketch I failed to emphasize enough the importance of establishing a staff group at an international institution charged with the collective task of improving analytical knowledge about international macroeconomic interactions and diffusing that knowledge more widely. Staff support of that type, backed up by an international epistemic community, is a necessary precondition for progress of other sorts.

The IMF, or perhaps a combination of the IMF, OECD, and the World Bank, is the most logical institutional locus for this staff support for strengthened multilateral surveillance. An inferior alternative would be to establish an explicit secretariat for the G-7 and to locate the analytical staff support as part of that secretariat.[18] Several keen observers of international consultations argue for more active use of the IMF and its staff rather than creation of a competing G-7 secretariat.[19] I share that judgment, both about general staff support for the backstopping and monitoring of G-7 consultations and in particular for the location of a special support staff charged with emphasizing the analytical foundations for international cooperation about macroeconomic stabilization policies. The support staff, both general and special, could be incorporated into the IMF Research Department or lodged in a newly created IMF department.

Analytical foundations are not a sexy subject for policymakers. But over the longer run, building more solid analytical foundations is the only reliable way to improve policy debate and render policy decisions more robust to error. Progress in model evaluation and model improvement is the ultimate answer to the problem of competing models (chapter 7).[20]

17. Bryant (1990a).
18. Ikenberry (1993) advocates this option.
19. See Dobson (1991, 1994); Solomon (1991); Fischer (1994); and Goldstein (1995).
20. Dobson, speaking about the multicountry macroeconomic models available for assessing the linkages among economies in an internally consistent manner, observes that "few ministers or deputies are enthusiastic about this kind of work. They tend to distrust quantitative sophistication of this kind, even as an aid to judgment, preferring to rely on their accumulated experience and back-of-the-envelope knowledge about linkages. But this

By tradition and comparative advantage, society looks to the academic community for new knowledge to be created and analytical foundations to be rebuilt. For the area of international cooperation about macroeconomic stabilization policies, as in general, the academic community can and should play an important role in improving analytical foundations. But policymakers cannot count solely on the academic community to make sufficient progress. Most academic researchers have limited knowledge of the ways in which unresolved analytical issues surface in policy discussions. Without sustained contact with the policy community, therefore, researchers are much less likely to condition their research in ways helpful to policymakers. Even more important, the structure of incentives and rewards for advancement in the academic community inhibit academics from giving priority attention to the analytical needs of policymakers. Fellow academics accord much higher praise, and give much greater weight in decisions about university appointments, to new theoretical wrinkles published in presitigious academic journals than to thoughtful efforts to refine empirical models by better application of existing analytical knowledge. Even the small group of academic economists who develop forecasting and simulation models usable for policy analysis are reluctant to devote their limited resources to model validation and model evaluation. Few academics hand out kudos to researchers who do the hard work of identifying the deficiencies in existing analytical frameworks or who carefully try to remedy inadequacies in existing data sources. To complement and supplement academic research, policymakers thus have a strong interest in making adequate resources available for officially commissioned research in support of strengthened multilateral surveillance.

Two types of research might be commissioned from support staff lodged in the IMF. One type, the responsibility mainly of the general support staff, would focus on topics figuring prominently in discussions about current policy or policy in the immediate future. Analyses of controversial aspects of the current economic outlook, for individ-

---

kind of work is needed to build a better shared technical understanding of the connections across economies, which eventually will feed upward into the deputies' briefings" (1991, p. 146). Solomon also points to the need for more explicit government support of "an ongoing research program on some of the unresolved analytical problems concerning coordination" (1991, p. 110). Fischer (1994, p. C-164) emphasizes the need for the IMF "to ensure that the analytic quality of its staff remains very high, and is indeed enhanced."

ual economies or the world system, would typically dominate the work. The second type, the responsibility of the special support staff, would have a longer horizon. Projects would be chosen because of their potential importance as building blocks for improved analytical foundations, not because they could be expected to have an immediate payoff.

Consider two examples of the longer-horizon type. First, the special support staff might be charged with careful evaluation of alternative rule-based national operating regimes and with alternative specifications of presumptive international guidelines for the regimes. This research would be, in effect, an intensification of the rule analysis discussed in chapter 4. The research would have to begin with quite simplified specifications of regimes and guidelines (for both monetary and fiscal policies) before more complex and realistic alternatives could be examined. Model evaluations and comparisons would inevitably be at the core of this work.

Second, the special support staff might be tasked with defining and estimating alternative concepts of equilibrium exchange rates and of equilibrium interest rates (national and global). What normative and modeling assumptions have to be specified to identify an exchange rate deemed to be in "equilibrium"? Essentially the same analytical issues are at stake if policymakers wish to identify when a nation's exchange rate is "misaligned" or "overvalued" or "undervalued." How can policymakers tell when a nation's real interest rate (or "the global" real interest rate) is too high or too low? Under what circumstances might a policymaker conclude that an exchange rate or an interest rate should be judged "excessively variable"?

Analysts have great difficulty in supplying helpful, nontautological answers to these questions. A carefully defined equilibrium rate must be characterized as a dynamic time path rather than a single value. Any specific calculation of an equilibrium path necessarily makes use of normative assumptions and therefore cannot be "neutral" about policymakers' goals. Moreover, estimates of equilibrium paths, for exchange rates or interest rates, are inescapably contingent on the particular theoretical or empirical model(s) in the context of which the estimates are made. Because estimates are both goal contingent and model contingent, in principle a multiplicity of useful calculations of equilibrium paths may exist. Analysts and policymakers have only begun to clarify the relevant concepts and empirical procedures, despite their clear importance for national policy decisions and international cooperation.[21]

My major emphasis is on analytical research by a strengthened IMF staff, which would facilitate more effective international consultations. But there is also some scope for improving the public release of macroeconomic analysis already conducted by the IMF, OECD, BIS, and World Bank. For example, copious macroeconomic analysis by the IMF staff of developments within particular countries could usefully be shared with a wider public. Greater outside scrutiny could improve the analysis itself and could raise the quality of domestic policy debate. Confidentiality for certain reports and discussions of course needs to be maintained. There is a minor risk that the quality and frankness of some analysis could decline if it had to be made publicly available. But I share the views of Stanley Fischer and Morris Goldstein that more transparency would strengthen rather than weaken the IMF.[22] Analogous points apply to many parts of the macroeconomic analyses at the OECD, BIS, and World Bank that are not currently placed in the public domain.

Collection and publication of statistical data, for national economies and for the global economy, is another collective good now supplied in some degree by international institutions but which will always require improvement and rethinking. Even within countries the quality and availability of data leave much to be desired. As regional economies and the world economy become still more integrated, the demand for reliable and consistently compiled data will increase further. International institutions must play a catalytic role in meeting this need.

---

21. Preferably, the general concept of equilibrium paths for exchange rates and interest rates should not by definition exclude certain types of policy action nor embody certain policy goals to the exclusion of others. The current status of analytical understanding about equilibrium exchange rates can be reviewed in the volume edited by John Williamson (1994); see especially the essay by Stanley Black, "On the Concept and Usefulness of the Equilibrium Rate of Exchange," the essay by a group of IMF staff on "The Robustness of Equilibrium Exchange Rate Calculations to Alternative Assumptions and Methodologies," and Williamson's own contributions.

22. Fischer (1994); Goldstein (1995). Prior to 1994, virtually all of the background reports, papers, and staff appraisals associated with Article IV consultations with individual countries were treated as confidential. In the fall of 1994, the IMF helpfully began to make publicly available some of the less sensitive documents associated with Article IV consultations, for example the staff reviews known as *Recent Economic Developments*.

The flow data available for the capital accounts of balances of payments and the corresponding stock data for nations' external-asset and external-liability positions are a salient but little emphasized example. For studying a variety of analytical questions in macroeconomics and finance for open economies, analysts require much better data on these cross-border relationships. In principle, one requires a breakdown of the balance sheets of financial institutions in all the important national jurisdictions, cross-classified by currency of denomination, residence of customer, and type of customer. Better data are certainly needed for cross-border security transactions and the corresponding stock asset and liability positions. Because off-balance sheet items such as futures, swaps, and other derivatives have become increasingly important, one needs substantial information on them as well. Ideally, over time international institutions would compile better quality and more comprehensive aggregates—national, regional, and global—for these data. Progress would gradually be made toward the ultimate objective of compiling a set of flow-of-funds accounts, consistent with national income accounts, for the world as a whole. The actual availability of such financial data falls very short of what is desirable in principle. Only a handful of countries have well-developed flow-of-funds accounts; and for them, the cross-border aspects are weakest. Although some potential building blocks are assembled at the BIS, the IMF, the OECD, and the World Bank, policymakers have so far given little thought to these data issues at the world systemic level.[23]

The primary impetus for enhanced analytical support for multilateral surveillance will have to come from policymakers and their advisers. But in a modest way there exists an epistemic community of individuals outside of governments and international organizations—for example, in academic institutions—who also try to advance theoretical and empirical knowledge about cross-border macroeconomic interactions. Members of this community also hope to, for example, evaluate alternative rule-based national operating regimes and alternative specifications of presumptive international guidelines. They too aspire to estimate equilibrium paths for exchange rates and interest rates. Far-sighted policymakers have a clear interest in nurturing this epistemic community, encouraging it to play an active role in develop-

23. Bryant (1991b).

ing analytical knowledge and applying that knowledge to international consultations.

A Longer-Run Vision

For the still longer run, how might international cooperation for macroeconomic policies be improved if national policymakers were to have the benefit of enhanced analytical support, both within national governments and from a secretariat located within the IMF? With the precondition of improved analytical knowledge satisfied, considerably more ambitious consultations and attempts at policy coordination would become possibilities. The evolutionary vision having the greatest appeal to me would have the following elements.[24]

One strand in the vision would extend, and deepen, the research of the IMF special support staff on analytical foundations. I have already stressed the need for and potential benefits of this activity. Like the refinement of statistical data, this activity must be a continuing obligation of the staffs of international institutions as far into the future as our imaginations can extend.

A second strand would entail gradual intensification of ongoing (lower-level) international cooperation about macroeconomic stabilization policies. Intergovernmental consultations about the current world economic outlook, backstopped by the international secretariat responsible for administrative and analytical support (the IMF general support staff), would be augmented. As a result, governments would be helped much more than at present to identify potentially fruitful opportunities for activist coordination.

Each national government participating in ongoing consultations about the current world economic situation would submit periodic projections of a "baseline outlook" to the international staff secretariat. The frequency of the projection "rounds" and meetings associated

24. Several studies already referenced, including Dobson (1991, 1994), Solomon (1991), and Goldstein (1995), have made recommendations for strengthening international macroeconomic cooperation. See also Artis and Ostry (1986) and Bretton Woods Commission (1994). Crockett (1989) reviews the roles of international institutions in supporting and monitoring international macroeconomic cooperation. My aspirations here are more ambitious than the recommendations in those other studies because I refer to a more distant period in the future and because I make the optimistic working assumption that cooperative efforts can rest on a stronger analytical foundation.

with them could vary but might presumptively be twice or three times a year.

At a minimum, each of the G-7 governments and each of the G-7 central banks would be involved. The nature of the consultations and cooperation *within* each country, involving the fiscal authority, the central bank, and other government agencies, would of course vary across the participating countries. Delicate, controversial issues of central-bank independence and the allocation of responsibilities for economic policy within governments have inhibited a deeper involvement of central banks in G-7 consultations. But more extensive involvement by the central banks would greatly improve the quality and relevance of the consultations. A key place for improving within-nation coordination is to develop strengthened interactions between the fiscal authority and the central bank in the preparation of the baseline outlook. Possibly, although not preferably, a nation's fiscal authority and central bank could submit separately prepared versions of the baseline outlook.[25]

The baseline outlook prepared by each national government would either assume "no change" in the nation's macroeconomic policies (no departures from policies presently in force) or alternatively could incorporate policy changes already decided upon or very likely to be made. Each national projection would be derived with the aid of one or more analytical frameworks (models) that try to be internally consistent. Each government, moreover, would be willing to—and would—exchange information about its models and projection methods. An individual government would concentrate most on projecting the key macroeconomic variables pertaining to its own economy. But each government would also be free to submit projections for other economies if it chose to do so.

The supporting international secretariat would also provide its own baseline projection of the outlook for each major country or region. The analytical support staff in the secretariat would make its own models and projection methods transparent to national governments. And it would function as a clearinghouse for the exchange of models and projections among governments.[26]

25. Note that this focus on interactions within each national government suggests the likely inappropriateness of analyzing each government as a unitary actor (chapter 5)!

26. The IMF's *World Economic Outlook* and the *OECD Economic Outlook* as published in the early 1990s are prototypes for the baseline outlooks of the international secretariat.

A wide range of quantity and price macroeconomic variables—for domestic real sectors, domestic financial sectors, balances of payments, and international markets—would be projected and reported in each baseline outlook. Some projections would be made for higher-frequency (monthly) data as well as for quarterly and annual data. Those preparing the projections would employ best-practice analytical techniques to make the projections for each frequency internally consistent. The actual instruments of each nation's monetary and fiscal policies and, of course, the ultimate-target variables of national policies, would feature most prominently. But key intermediate, indicator variables would also be included.

Treatment of exchange rates in these projections would be, no less so than now, a delicate and controversial issue. A politically safe approach would be to have all participants assume that real effective exchange rates (or, within arrangements such as the European Monetary System, nominal exchange rates) would remain unchanged from the values prevailing in a period just prior to preparation of the projections. If mutual trust were high enough and confidentiality could be maintained during the projection process, it would be analytically informative to follow a second approach as well in which the paths of key exchange rates were projected endogenously.

The international secretariat would play, and would be strongly encouraged to play, a key analytical role in the evaluation of the different versions of the baseline outlook. For example, the secretariat would prepare a systematic comparison of the new baselines prepared for the current round, pointing out inconsistencies among the different nations' and the secretariat's versions. The secretariat would also systematically compare the ex ante outlooks submitted in the preceding round with updated information about ex post outcomes. An integral element of the staff support associated with this process would be the identification of analytical puzzles and gaps in knowledge that warrant further clarification and research.

Another vital component of the evolutionary process of international consultations would be "what-if simulations." Such simulations, judiciously chosen to shed light on issues of current relevance,

---

Similarly, the monitoring surveillance in G-7 consultations in the mid-1990s contains the seeds of the plant I envisage here. For descriptions of the 1990s monitoring surveillance, see Goldstein (1992, 1995) and Crockett (1989).

would examine the consequences of changing this or that policy instrument. Similarly, simulations would be prepared asking, What if such and such a nonpolicy shock were to occur? Changes in macroeconomic variables resulting from these hypothetical policy and nonpolicy alterations would be measured relative to the baseline outlook. Such what-if scenarios would be prepared, at a minimum, by the international secretariat. Ideally, national governments would also prepare them, especially for changes in their own policy instruments, but even for changes in other governments' policy instruments and for various nonpolicy shocks. Differences in models would of course lead to differences in the answers to the what-if questions. No attempt would be made to suppress differences attributable to model uncertainty. On the contrary, the range of differences would be the subject of attention in the consultations and would be important grist for the mill of the analytical support group, suggesting problems with the differing models or properties needing clarification.

Periodic meetings of the national policymakers, and preparatory meetings of their deputies, would typically examine the baseline-outlook projections, some of the most relevant what-if scenarios, and the associated evaluations prepared by the secretariat. No less important, the discussions would involve frank exchanges of information about the individual governments' goals. Efforts would be made to classify differences in the baseline projections and what-if scenarios according to whether they were due to differences in identification of initial conditions (current positions of the national economies), differences in national goals, differences in preferred models, or differences in assumptions about expected future nonpolicy shocks.

The cooperative exercise envisaged here could sometimes give rise to an activist coordination of policies. Examination of the what-if scenarios would in any event keep the participating governments alert to possibilities for mutually beneficial coordination at the same time as they focused on differences among models and the risks of making errors because of model uncertainty. If the process worked well, a creative tension would be maintained and participants would continually try to balance beneficial opportunities against the possibilities for counterproductive consequences (chapter 6). In effect, lookouts would be posted to watch for market failures and government failures alike.

A plausible by-product of this strengthened process for ongoing consultations could be some convergence in the analytical understanding brought by policymakers to the consultations. Preferred models for describing national economies and cross-border spillovers could become less diverse. Preferences for specific rule-based national operating regimes might converge somewhat. One can even imagine that some convergence could eventually take place in the way government officials articulate national goals and identify goals that are commonly shared.

A rudimentary variant of the long-run vision outlined here could conceivably be tried in the medium run. In limited respects, it is even possible to interpret G-7 discussions in the 1990s as hesitantly groping in this direction. The most important ingredient missing from actual experience, however, has been the supporting role of a proactive international secretariat charged with catalyzing the process. Putting greater muscle into such a process will of course be contingent on continuing advances in the underlying analytical knowledge.

If we try to peer into the very distant future, we can imagine international economic cooperation on a scale not discussed in this book. The possible creation of worldwide federalist supranational institutions could become a subject for debate. The explicit harmonization of some national economic policies might be politically feasible and hence would require evaluation of the associated costs and benefits. Seen in terms of the maps portrayed in figures 2-2 and 2-3 in chapter 2, regions of the world and the world as a whole might conceivably have moved, or be in the process of moving, substantially further in an eastward and southerly direction.

Coordination of national monetary policies might evolve toward a "world monetary policy" in an increasingly integrated world financial system. Issues of whether to have a common currency (or a few common regional currencies), and how to manage exchange rates among the separate currencies still in existence, would of course become paramount. Fascinating institutional issues would gain salience: for example, the possible evolution of the IMF (or an entirely new institution?) toward a world central bank and the political independence of that bank from supranational federalist institutions and from national governments.[27]

27. Cooper (1984, 1990) and Eichengreen's Integrating National Economies book (1994) raise some of these issues.

"Fiscal policies" in that far-distant time would be even more complex and multilayered than in the world of the 1990s. One would still find national governments deciding upon and implementing national budgets. Even in such conditions, we would not speak of the explicit harmonization of national (and local) budgetary policies but rather of their coordination (chapter 2). Many layers of the fiscal policies would still be subject to the presumption in favor of subsidiarity, accommodating diversity in preferences, and tying governance and the provision of public goods to different political jurisdictions in which the differing preferences were manifested. But of course analysis and debate would also have to focus on the budgets of the regional and supranational institutions and their interdependence with lower-level fiscal policies and with world monetary policy.

Even to allude to these longer-run issues is to underscore the fact that they will arise only in the distant rather than the near future. For the topic of macroeconomic stabilization policies, therefore, it seems prudent for the time being not to speculate in detail about what lies ahead that far down the road. It is more productive to focus aspirations on the short and medium runs, on what might be accomplished during the next decade or two. Within that time frame, the key goal should be for major governments to perceive more clearly their collective interest in establishing adequate analytical support for international macroeconomic cooperation and to give supporting groups sufficient resources and authority to foster that collective interest.

Chapter 10

Summary

THIS BOOK analyzes a central issue for integrating national economies: when should national governments cooperate in making decisions about their macroeconomic stabilization policies and, if they do so, how ambitious should that cooperation be? The varieties of cooperation and basic analytical concepts are identified in chapter 2. Three different analytical perspectives are then brought to bear in subsequent chapters: the traditional policy-optimization analysis favored by economists, rule analysis of international regime environments, and the institutionalist analysis developed by scholars in international relations and political science.

Virtually all forms of intergovernmental cooperation entail consultations and exchanges of information. In most circumstances, such consultations and exchanges are widely—and, I believe, correctly—thought to be beneficial. More ambitious forms of cooperation, however, involve *coordination* of national monetary and fiscal policies. Much of the book is concerned with such coordination, not merely with the milder and less controversial forms of cooperation.

A fundamental rationale supports the case for coordinating national stabilization policies. Because economic integration across national borders has generated a growing variety and intensity of collective-action problems with international dimensions, furthermore, the force of that rationale has been increasing during recent decades.

The essence of the rationale is straightforward and can be restated simply. Decentralized national decisions that fail to take into account the cross-border spillovers from policy actions can produce outcomes that are inferior to more efficient outcomes attainable through informed collective action. The inferior outcomes are examples of situations in which negative externalities lead to market failures. If governments consult and bargain with one another intelligently and cooperatively, they may be able to identify mutually beneficial adjustments of their policy instruments that offset the market failures and thereby permit their nations to reach higher levels of welfare.

Governmental efforts to coordinate policies, however, will not invariably be successful. In international coordination as in all other areas of economics and politics, government intervention intended to remedy a market failure can be counterproductive. Chapter 6 identifies circumstances in which coordination efforts might lower rather than raise welfare.

My personal eclecticism leads me to give more weight to the potential benefits of attempted coordination than to the potential risks. On the whole, international cooperation among governments can reasonably be expected—in many, though admittedly not all, circumstances—to advance the common interests of their citizens. The presumption in favor of subsidiarity, stressed in chapter 2, is a safeguard inhibiting government officials from trying to coordinate stabilization policies with excessive zeal. When national governments respect subsidiarity as a guideline, actual coordination will be attempted only when strong evidence is accumulated suggesting that spillover externalities are causing major difficulties and that a feasible adjustment of national policies seems likely to improve the macroeconomic outlook significantly.

Can coordination of macroeconomic policies yield large gains in welfare? For reasons given in chapter 3, the existing theoretical and empirical evidence is, unfortunately, inconclusive. Estimates of the potential gains are sensitively dependent on the specific model and the ancillary assumptions used in a researcher's analysis. Although a majority of researchers tend to the view that the incremental gains from coordination are modest, further research is required to produce a reliable consensus.

Coordination of stabilization policies can be activist. That is, policymakers can exercise discretionary flexibility to alter their instrument settings and to try to identify bargains with other nations' policymakers. Alternatively, coordination can focus on rule-based national operating regimes. In that case, international cooperation comes into play mainly to establish the presumptive guidelines, agreed to internationally, that condition the rule-like constraints followed by each national government.

Some proponents of rules rather than discretion regard rules as a first-best approach to policy. Other proponents believe that activist full coordination is not feasible and that rule-based coordination, as a second best, can emulate some of the favorable consequences that would be achieved if full coordination were feasible. I see merit in both analytical approaches to coordination issues and do not rank rules as preferable to discretion, or vice versa. Much more research needs to be done on both activist and rule-based approaches. Indeed, differences of view about rules and discretion—with the associated themes of commitment, credibility, and time consistency—are among the most salient and controversial issues about all aspects of the conduct of macroeconomic stabilization policies. The debate about the domestic and international aspects is certain to continue well into the next century.

A major insight of institutionalist analysis is that intergovernmental cooperation, when most manifest, can be explained as regime maintenance and satisficing stabilization, and especially as the management of actual or latent crises. The presumption of diffuse reciprocity means that governments agree to cooperate because they plausibly expect to benefit over many periods on many issues, but not necessarily every period on every issue. Institutionalist analysis also calls attention to multiple-agent interactions within national governments that are ignored when national governments are assumed to make decisions as unitary actors. The institutionalist perspective is a complement to rather than a substitute for the policy-optimization analysis and rule analysis favored by economists. Insights about cooperation and coordination derived from all three analytical perspectives can be combined to generate a balanced and more thoughtful understanding (chapter 5).

This book argues, controversially, that analytical uncertainty about the functioning of the world economy is the single greatest impediment to international macroeconomic cooperation. Hence I stress that the *feasibility* of cooperation and coordination, not their desirability, should be the primary focus of attention in policy analysis. Policymakers considering coordination should use all the information available to them about cross-border interactions. But they should not try to suppress differences in view attributable to different analytical models. It makes sense for policymakers engaged in international consultations to try to identify mutual adjustments in national policies that promise potential gains, as judged by any of the analytical models preferred by individual participating governments. The greater the consensus among differing models about the potential gains, the more seriously should policymakers consider implementing the mutual policy adjustments. Because of model uncertainty, however, there can be no assurance that such policy adjustments will exist in any particular circumstances.

An improved analytical understanding of macroeconomic interactions among national economies is a prerequisite for making progress on virtually every significant macroeconomic issue, positive or normative, confronting national policymakers. This improved understanding is inescapably necessary for more successful international coordination of stabilization policies, whether activist or rule based. That conclusion leads directly to this book's modest, practical recommendations for facilitating enhanced intergovernmental cooperation in the future (chapter 9). Major governments need to recognize more clearly their common interest in strengthening the analytical support for (what has come to be labeled) multilateral surveillance. Such recognition should in turn lead governments to provide the staff of international institutions with sufficient resources and authority to foster that common interest.

Note that my modest recommendations fully respect the presumption in favor of subsidiarity. For the short and medium runs, I do not envisage a significant strengthening of centralized authority for the IMF or other international institutions. My aspiration is merely to strengthen the ability of national policymakers to identify opportunities for self-interested mutual adjustment of their macroeconomic policy decisions. Consultations and bargaining would be multilateral, but decisions would continue to be decentralized and unilateral.

Comments

Takatoshi Ito

Ralph Bryant's book presents a grand survey and an original thesis on policy coordination. As an author of many studies on policy coordination in the past, he is most suited for this subject. My comments are not comprehensive but focused on several aspects of policy coordination that, I think, shed different kinds of light on this general subject.

Theory of International Policy Coordination

Policy coordination can be justified by the existence of externalities—in effect "market failures"—that can occur when individual countries ignore the effects of their policies on other countries. Thus if countries conduct their monetary, fiscal, and exchange rate policies independently, it is relatively easy to show that the resulting outcome (known technically as the Nash equilibrium) can be inferior to that attainable through coordination (a cooperative solution). However, the existence of externalities does not necessarily mean that coordination is better, unless the governments involved have complete information and behave optimally in devising coordination. Even if market failure exists, coordination among governments may not improve the situation. Government failure may occur, for example, because a govern-

Takatoshi Ito is senior adviser in the research department of the International Monetary Fund. The views expressed here are those of the author and do not necessarily reflect those of the International Monetary Fund.

ment may not act on behalf of the welfare of its private sector but may pursue its own agenda. Negotiation costs may not be negligible. (Cautions on the possibility of counterproductive coordination are given in chapter 6.) In theory, there is no definite answer to the question of whether policy coordination is desirable or not. The answer depends on relative sizes of market failure and government failure.

Economic Integration and Policy Coordination

The world (at least among industrialized countries) has become more and more integrated. Trade barriers have been lowered and technology has made information, transportation, and transactions costs much less expensive than before. One way to understand issues of policy coordination in a more integrated world is by differentiating private sector responses from policy responses. There is little disagreement about what integration does to economic activities of the private sector. More integration will lead to efficient international allocation of resources. For example, capital (and to some extent, labor) will flow from countries with low returns to those with high returns (good opportunities). This will equalize interest rates (adjusted for expected exchange rate changes) among integrated countries. This theoretical prediction is in fact testable.

An interesting question is whether more integration requires more or less policy coordination. To answer this question, it is better to differentiate the perspective of small countries from that of large countries. For small countries, which take the world interest rate and other variables as given, more integration with the world economy most likely will lead to the loss of independent policies. When capital controls are abolished, monetary policy of other countries does affect capital inflows and outflows, which in turn affect the domestic interest rate level and the exchange rate. Hence, benefits from coordination will increase. For example, if a small country adopts a fixed exchange rate system with perfect capital mobility, the monetary policy is automatically set so that coordination is perfect, though rather automatic (without negotiation).

In deciding macroeconomic policies in a more integrated world, would large countries become more "careful" about how their policies might affect smaller countries? For example, would the United States, Germany, or Japan consider how changes in their interest rates might affect payments of the debtor nations who had borrowed at the short-term interest rates, such as the London Interbank Offer Rate? Probably not. In that sense, the integration of smaller countries with the world is unilaterally affecting small countries but not large countries. In other words, integration may actually make smaller countries adjust to large countries. (This automatic adjustment is probably not the kind of policy coordination that is a concern here. But this simple example shows the difference between integration and coordination.) However, most likely integration is viewed as good even when (or precisely because) room to use discretionary policy becomes smaller.

International (active) policy coordination is usually discussed in the framework of large countries: an action in one (large) country affects the environment of another (large) country, and vice versa. Realistically, large countries here are the United States, Germany (or Germany-led Europe), and Japan. As large countries are integrated through trade and investment, more channels of international spillovers (externalities) open up. Large countries are better off coordinating their acts because of bilateral influences on each other. We have witnessed a surge in interest in policy coordination in the 1980s because of the combination of a rise of non-U.S. economies to a status that influences the U.S. economy and a realization that there are gains to be made from coordination.

Hence, the degree of integration and the degree of coordination may most likely be positively correlated (see chapters 2 and 3).

The United States as the Hegemon

Right after World War II, the United States had a large share of world production and was clearly a dominant country. The United States, however, should be credited, with other allies, for creating various international organizations—such as the International Monetary Fund and the World Bank—that foster international coordination. During the cold war, economic and international security provided by the United States was key to the "western" countries. For better or worse, the United States of America has been a dominant actor (hegemon) in the international relationship.

From the end of World War II to the mid-1960s, the United States was the only "large country": whatever the United States did influenced the rest of the world, but actions by any country in the rest of the world rarely affected the U.S. economy in any significant way. "Externalities," if any, were essentially unilateral, and the international monetary system was essentially based on the U.S. dollar, which was convertible to gold. All other industrial countries were essentially "small." It would be fair to say that the United States exercised the "hegemon" power in a manner that helped economic development in Europe and Japan. In the late 1940s and 1950s, economic aid provided by the United States was enormously helpful for the economic recovery in Japan and Europe. Only a little coordination was required in the relationship between the United States and the rest of the industrial countries.

However, the balance of economic power gradually shifted out of the United States. From the mid- to late 1960s, how to maintain the Bretton Woods system (fixed exchange rates to the gold convertible U.S. dollar) became probably the first test of coordination. After some jolt to the system in the late 1960s, the Bretton Woods system finally collapsed (a suspension of conversion from dollars to gold, devaluation of the dollar, and import surcharges) in August 1971. An attempt to restore the fixed exchange rate system at new parities, the Smithsonian agreement of December 1971, did not survive long. Japan and Germany went free floating in the spring of 1973. The need for policy coordination had become greater and greater as U.S. dominance waned.

Coordination in Practice: Is the United States Still Unique?

The second half of the 1980s was the heyday of international policy coordination. The Plaza Agreement, Louvre Accord (both on the exchange rate policy), and frequent concerted interest rate adjustments can be cited as evidence for considerable enthusiasm for coordination among the major industrial countries. There was a popular notion among economists and politicians that the global economy would be better managed when the large countries (say, Group of Five) cooperated. The Group of Five economic summit started in 1975. (As Bryant correctly points out, most successful coordination is "episodic.")

However, even in the 1980s, among the Japanese and Europeans, caution prevailed because it was thought that unless the United States joined the game, international coordination made little sense.

Policymakers in Japan and Europe would point out that the rules of the game can be altered when the United States considers the rule not suited to the world (or to the United States). For example, in the 1940s the International Trade Organization was not initiated because the U.S. Congress did not ratify the necessary treaty. And in 1971 the U.S. government unilaterally abandoned the Bretton Woods exchange rate system by suspending the convertibility of the U.S. dollar into gold, thereby effectively devaluing the dollar against European currencies and the Japanese yen. That action was a major departure from the international monetary regime centered on the U.S. dollar and was not at all a result of policy coordination. (The United States would counterargue that Germany and Japan had not revalued earlier.) In 1978 Japan and Germany felt that they were too little to be "locomotives" to pull the industrial economies, but reluctantly agreed to implement expansionary policies. In the first half of the 1980s, Japan and Europe felt that they were pressured by the United States to change various policies (not only macroeconomic but regulatory) in order to reduce the U.S. trade deficits, despite the fact, which the U.S. administration at the time denied, that U.S. trade deficits were caused by high U.S. government deficits and resulting high interest rates. In the late 1980s, Japan experienced overheated asset markets (known as the bubble economy), but some of the blame is placed on the Louvre Accord "targeting" the exchange rate.

In sum, from the Japanese and European viewpoints, international policy coordination is only possible when the United States wants it. In that sense, the United States remains the largest of large countries. It implies that, in a theoretical framework, the situation may be modeled as the leader-follower game, rather than a cooperative game or a Nash equilibrium. This aspect could be emphasized more strongly in the discussion.

Whither Coordination?

In the 1990s the enthusiasm for international coordination has waned somewhat. It may be because the exchange rate coordination (Louvre Accord among G-3 and EMS in Europe) has become less effective, if not broken down, or because challenges by theoretical and simulation models became convincing (see chapter 6). A more positive way of understanding this reverse swing in the pendulum is that getting one's house in order first is more important and often more difficult than international policy coordination. When one country is running large fiscal deficits, coordinating through the exchange rate or monetary policy becomes very difficult. If some interest groups capture tax policy, arguing the virtue of international policy coordination becomes very difficult.

In some cases, policy coordination (for example, anchoring the exchange rate) exerts enough pressure on domestic political forces to put them on track. In some countries (especially Japan), foreign pressure (especially from the United States), acted to break political deadlock. But, more often, domestic interest groups capture political power in order to change economic policy in a way that becomes counterproductive not only to domestic objectives but to international coordination. Even if a central bank is poised to coordinate with other central banks, a domestic situation, such as Parliament's (Congress) cutting taxes without cutting expenditures, might prevent the government from cooperating internationally. One way to avoid political capture is by setting rules for coordination rather than promoting activist coordination. (This is a parallel to domestic monetary policy debate and is mentioned in chapter 2.) This kind of problem can be, and has been, analyzed to some extent in the literature of two-stage games. The domestic game (such as a game between pro-fiscal expansion versus balanced budget) has to be settled before any stance toward international coordination is considered, while (an anticipation of) international constraints also alter the rules of domestic games.

In sum, the success of international coordination crucially hinges on sound domestic macroeconomic policies. Difficulties in getting domestic policies right in the 1990s for various political reasons and rather synchronous, cyclical downturns among the United States, Japan, and the United Kingdom (followed by continental European countries) are partly to blame for a cooler reception of international coordination among large countries. Some critics may argue that the United States has turned inward. However, undoubtedly sometime in the future, when domestic situations in large countries drive the governments toward coordination, policy coordination will come back onto the international policy agenda.

Paul R. Masson

It is a pleasure to comment on this important book, which is the latest of a long series of contributions that Ralph Bryant has made in several related areas, in particular, in multicountry modeling of macroeconomic spillovers, in the analysis of the effects of financial integration, and in policy coordination itself. Bryant has written a very interesting and readable survey of the literature in this area, with a focus appropriately personal to the author. I agree with much of this focus, but I do have some small quibbles with details and skepticism about a few of his recommendations, even though some of my comments on an earlier draft have led to changes in the final version.

Clearly, Bryant has a strong prior belief that international macroeconomic policy coordination is a good thing. Coordination should emulate the policy bargains reached at the 1978 Bonn summit, at which Germany and Japan agreed to a fiscal expansion and the United States agreed to put its energy policy in order, or the Plaza Accord, which produced policies to correct the overvalued dollar. Policy coordination should be activist (discretionary), rather than based on mechanistic rules, and should be continuous rather than episodic, as it tends to be now. Though Bryant denies this in the book, it is nevertheless natural to assume that progress means moving in his diagrams from the northwest to the southeast—away from national autonomy with policy based on simple, rigid rules to highly activist discretionary coordination in a global federalist system.

To my mind, there are good reasons (many are mentioned in the book) why macroeconomic policy coordination is episodic. The gains in crisis periods can be great, as Atish Ghosh and I have argued, and the uncertainty in these periods is precisely what provides the incentive to coordinate, rather than being an obstacle to coordination. However, crisis periods are fortunately few, and in normal times policymakers are probably best advised to devote their energies to putting their own houses in order, rather than to using international agreements (or the excuse of the lack of one) to postpone needed domestic action. The model simulation results cited by Bryant no doubt reflect the normal tranquil periods and hence find only modest

Paul R. Masson is assistant director of the research department of the International Monetary Fund. The views expressed here are those of the author and do not necessarily reflect those of the International Monetary Fund.

gains from coordination. However, I would certainly believe that the payoff from coordination can at times be extraordinarily great; for instance, one could reasonably argue that international coordination could have significantly moderated, if not avoided, the Great Depression, while even if governments had recognized the problem, uncoordinated expansions in individual countries would have been hard to achieve and much less effective.

Bryant argues, as others have, that the mechanism of coordination must be in place even if not currently needed, just as the firefighters playing cards while waiting for a call are also serving a purpose. Moreover, continuous policy cooperation also means much sharing of information that may in fact be as useful as explicit coordination. I would generally agree. Nevertheless, I would place more emphasis than Bryant does on international codes of conduct than on discretionary policy bargains. And furthermore, I would be less sanguine than he that sharing information is in everyone's best interest, so that it is sufficient just to call for more sharing. It may be necessary to twist governments' arms to get them to provide information as part of a broader set of understandings.

The trouble with discretionary bargains is that they are likely to be concluded by a small subset of the players—for instance, by the G-7 or even just the United States and Japan—and hence there is no guarantee that those not a party to the agreement will be better off. No doubt there are good examples where the rest of the world gains—for instance, the correction of an overvalued currency without a financial crisis may be in everyone's interest—but this need not always be the case. Discretionary bargains for stabilization policy are only feasible for a small number of participants; in contrast, agreements to establish the international rules of the game, because they are not linked to temporary cyclical considerations, can be negotiated over longer periods and hence can include a much wider set of countries—such as the recently concluded Uruguay Round agreement. This may be a more promising avenue than hoping that discretionary policy bargains may become more prevalent and continuous; such bargains may be essential at infrequent times of crisis but should not be the common fare of policymakers. In this context, I think that the principle of subsidiarity should, as is increasingly understood in the European Union, guide the creation of institutions: the rules of the game should be set up such that powers are exercised at the lowest level possible, thus permitting them to be tailored to individual circumstances, whether national, regional, or local. This principle would be an antidote to the preconception that more global decisionmaking is necessarily better, and it could have received more attention in the book.

Given that Bryant believes in the value of coordination and cooperation more broadly, he is anxious to cite evidence in its favor. For instance, he puts some weight on model simulations that show that acting myopically is significantly worse than acting strategically with knowledge of other governments' actions—hence that exchange of information among governments is a good thing, whether or not they coordinate. Unfortunately, these simulations do not really allow one to separate the information available publicly from that exchanged among governments (presumably, on a confidential basis), and hence to evaluate the gains from this form of international cooperation. Moreover, it is not always true that everyone has an incentive to share information—as should be obvious to anyone who has ever attempted to bargain over the purchase of a house or a car. The example that Atish Ghosh and I used in our book[1] was the case of information on exchange market intervention; if governments do not have the same objectives, they may want to disguise the amount (or direction) of their intervention from one another (as well as from the public). Other examples can readily be found: if one country wants to resist pressures to stimulate the economy, it may have incentives to emphasize current data (and official forecasts) that show that its economy is growing fast, that its trade surplus is declining, and that inflationary fires are being stoked. Bryant now acknowledges this possibility in his book but gives it little credence. Bryant also argues that uncertainty about the effects of policy implies that the emphasis in the academic literature on reneging is misplaced, since it is hard to define reneging in this context. But this uncertainty is precisely why policymakers— who after all are politicians—think they can do it and get away with it.

The reason that such attempts to shade the facts can occur is that great uncertainty exists, so that verifiability is impossible. Governments' forecasts will be wrong because of a host of unforeseen events, whose contribution to the forecasting error will be hard to establish, and policymakers will miss their targets because of these events and

---

1. *Economic Cooperation in an Uncertain World* (Oxford: Basil Blackwell, 1994).

also because of the vagaries of parliamentary approval and policy implementation—as well as possibly the absence of a serious attempt to hit their targets. Bryant also stresses uncertainty and describes its various manifestations: the position of the economy, policymakers' preferences, and the effects of policies. I agree with much of what is said, which draws on my book with Ghosh. However, I would not go so far as to say, as Bryant does, that "'model uncertainty' . . . is the single greatest impediment to sound policymaking within national governments and to successful international cooperation for macro-economic policies."

Bryant discusses extensively how we can evaluate, compare, and improve models—especially the international models that could serve as a basis for coordination. I would stress the inherent limitations of models—they are after all models, not the real thing. In that important sense, there is no "true model." Since they do not capture all aspects of reality, they are selective and tend to be adapted to particular issues. Clearly, important details will be left out, and aggregation problems ensure that the changing composition of the economy—different households or firms—will affect the model's parameters. Also, for Lucas critique reasons, they will change endogenously as a result of policy or other causes, unless we have modeled deep parameters—which even models with thousands of equations clearly will not have done. So policymakers are wise not to put all their eggs in these model baskets even if there are many of them.

References

Allison, Graham T. 1971. *Essence of Decision: Explaining the Cuban Missile Crisis.* Little, Brown.

Antholis, William John. 1993. *Liberal Democratic Theory and the Transformation of Sovereignty.* Ph.D. dissertation, Yale University.

Arrow, Kenneth J. 1963. "Uncertainty and the Welfare Economics of Medical Care." *American Economic Review* 53 (December): 941–73.

———. 1968. "The Economics of Moral Hazard: Further Comment." *American Economic Review* 58 (June): 537–39.

———. 1974. "Limited Knowledge and Economic Analysis." *American Economic Review* 64 (March): 1–10.

Artis, Michael, and Sylvia Ostry. 1986. *International Economic Policy Coordination.* Chatham House Papers 30, Royal Institute of International Affairs. London: Routledge & Kegan Paul.

Axelrod, Robert. 1984. *The Evolution of Cooperation.* Basic Books.

Backus, David, and John Driffill. 1985a. "Inflation and Reputation." *American Economic Review* 75 (June): 530–38.

———. 1985b. "Rational Expectations and Policy Credibility Following a Change in Regime." *Review of Economic Studies* 52 (April): 211–21.

Barro, Robert. 1986. "Reputation in a Model of Monetary Policy with Incomplete Information." *Journal of Monetary Economics* 17 (January): 3–20.

Barro, Robert, and David Gordon. 1983. "Rules, Discretion and Reputation in a Model of Monetary Policy." *Journal of Monetary Economics* 12 (July): 101–21.

Barry, Brian, and Russell Hardin, eds. 1982. *Rational Man and Irrational Society?: An Introduction and Sourcebook.* Beverly Hills, Calif.: Sage Publications.

Bator, Francis M. 1958. "The Anatomy of Market Failure." *Quarterly Journal of Economics* 72 (August): 351–79.

Baumol, William J., and Wallace E. Oates. 1975. *The Theory of Environmental Policy: Externalities, Public Outlays and the Quality of Life.* Prentice-Hall.

Bergsten, C. Fred, and John Williamson. 1994. "Is the Time Ripe for Target Zones or the Blueprint?" In Bretton Woods Commission, *Bretton Woods: Looking to the Future,* C21–C30. Washington: Bretton Woods Commission.

Blommestein, Hans J., ed. 1991. *The Reality of International Economic Policy Coordination.* Amsterdam: North-Holland.

Bosworth, Barry, and Gur Ofer. 1995. *Reforming Planned Economies in an Integrating World Economy.* Brookings.

Brainard, William. 1967. "Uncertainty and the Effectiveness of Policy." *American Economic Review* 57, *Papers and Proceedings* (May): 411–25.

Brandsma, Andries S., and Andrew Hughes Hallett. 1989. "The Design of Interdependent Policies with Incomplete Information." *Economic Modelling* 6 (October): 432–46.

Branson, William H., Jacob A. Frenkel, and Morris Goldstein, eds. 1990. *International Policy Coordination and Exchange Rate Fluctuations.* University of Chicago Press.

Brennan, Geoffrey L., and James M. Buchanan. 1977. "Towards a Tax Constitution for Leviathan." *Journal of Public Economics* 8 (December): 255–73.

Brennan, Geoffrey L., and James M. Buchanan. 1980. *The Power to Tax: Analytical Foundations of a Fiscal Constitution.* Cambridge University Press.

Bretton Woods Commission. 1994. *Bretton Woods: Looking to the Future.* Washington: Bretton Woods Commission.

Bryant, Ralph C. 1980. *Money and Monetary Policy in Interdependent Nations.* Brookings.

———. 1983. *Controlling Money: The Federal Reserve and Its Critics.* Brookings.

———. 1985. "Comment" on Marcus Miller and Mark Salmon, "Policy Coordination and Dynamic Games." In *International Economic Policy Coordination,* edited by Willem H. Buiter and Richard C. Marston, 213–19. Cambridge University Press.

———. 1987a. *International Financial Intermediation.* Brookings.

———. 1987b. "Intergovernmental Coordination of Economic Policies: An Interim Stocktaking." In *International Monetary Cooperation: Essays in Honor of Henry C. Wallich,* 4–15. Princeton Essay in International Finance 169. Princeton University, International Finance Section (December).

———. 1990a. "Comment" on Jeffrey Frankel, "Obstacles to Coordination, and a Consideration of Two Proposals to Overcome Them: International Nominal Targeting (INT) and the Hosomi Fund." In *International Policy Coordination and Exchange Rate Fluctuations,* edited by William Branson and others, 145–53. University of Chicago Press.

———. 1990b. "The Evolution of the International Monetary System: Where Next?" In *The Evolution of the International Monetary System: How Can Efficiency and Stability Be Attained?,* edited by Yoshio Suzuki, Junichi Miyake, and Mitsuaki Okabe, 15–38. University of Tokyo Press.

———. 1991a. "Model Representations of Japanese Monetary Policy," *Monetary and Economic Studies* 9 (Bank of Japan) (September): 11–61. (Available as Discussion Paper in International Economics 84, January 1991, Brookings).

————. 1991b. "Concluding Observations." In *International Economic Transactions: Issues in Measurement and Empirical Research*, edited by Peter Hooper and J. David Richardson, 476–83. Studies in Income and Wealth, vol. 55. University of Chicago Press for the National Bureau of Economic Research.

————. 1995. "International Cooperation in the Making of National Macroeconomic Policies: Where Do We Stand?" In *Understanding Interdependence: The Macroeconomics of the Open Economy*, edited by Peter B. Kenen, 391–447. Princeton University Press.

Bryant, Ralph C., and others, eds. 1989. *Macroeconomic Policies in an Interdependent World*. Brookings, Centre for Economic Policy Research, and International Monetary Fund.

Bryant, Ralph C., John F. Helliwell, and Peter Hooper. 1989. "Domestic and Cross-Border Consequences of U.S. Macroeconomic Policies." In *Macroeconomic Policies in an Interdependent World*, edited by Ralph C. Bryant and others, 59–115. Brookings, Centre for Economic Policy Research, and International Monetary Fund. (Unabridged version in Discussion Paper in International Economics 68, January 1989, Brookings).

Bryant, Ralph C., and others, eds. 1988. *Empirical Macroeconomics for Interdependent Economies*. Brookings.

Bryant, Ralph C., Gerald Holtham, and Peter Hooper, eds. 1988. *External Deficits and the Dollar: The Pit and the Pendulum*. Brookings.

Bryant, Ralph C., Peter Hooper, and Catherine L. Mann, eds. 1993. *Evaluating Policy Regimes: New Research in Empirical Macroeconomics*. Brookings.

Bryant, Ralph C., and Warwick J. McKibbin. 1994. "Macroeconomic Effects on Developing Economies of Shocks in the OECD: Evidence from Multicountry Models." Discussion Paper in International Economics 102. Brookings.

Bryant, Ralph C., and Richard Portes, eds. 1987. *Global Macroeconomics: Policy Conflict and Cooperation*. London: Macmillan for the Centre for Economic Policy Research.

Bryant, Ralph C., and Long Zhang. Forthcoming. "Intertemporal Fiscal Policy in Macroeconomic Models: Introduction and Major Alternatives." Discussion Paper in International Economics. Brookings.

Buiter, Willem H., and Richard C. Marston, eds. 1985. *International Economic Policy Coordination*. Cambridge University Press for the Center for Economic Policy Research and National Bureau of Economic Research.

Calvo, Guillermo. 1978. "On the Time Consistency of Optimal Policy in a Monetary Economy." *Econometrica* 46 (November): 1411–28.

Canzoneri, Matthew. 1985. "Monetary Policy Games and the Role of Private Information." *American Economic Review* 75 (December): 1056–70.

Canzoneri, Matthew, and Hali Edison. 1990. "A New Interpretation of the Coordination Problem and Its Empirical Significance." In *Monetary Aggregates and Financial Sector Behavior in Interdependent Economies*, edited by Peter Hooper, 399–433. Washington: Board of Governors of the Federal Reserve System.

Canzoneri, Matthew, and Jo Anna Gray. 1985. "Monetary Policy Games and the Consequences of Non-cooperative Behavior." *International Economic Review* 26 (October): 547–64.

Canzoneri, Matthew B., and Dale W. Henderson. 1991. *Monetary Policy in Interdependent Economies: A Game-Theoretic Approach.* MIT Press.

Canzoneri, Matthew, and Patrick Minford. 1988. "When International Policy Coordination Matters: An Empirical Analysis." *Applied Economics* 20 (September): 1137–54.

———. 1989. "Policy Interdependence: Does Strategic Behavior Pay? An Empirical Investigation Using the Liverpool World Model." In *Macroeconomic Policy and Economic Interdependence,* edited by Donald Hodgman and Geoffrey Wood, 158–79. St. Martin's Press.

Caporaso, James A. 1989. "Introduction: The State in Comparative and International Perspective." In *The Elusive State: International and Comparative Perspectives,* edited by Donald Hodgman and Geoffrey Wood, 7–16. Newbury Park, Calif.: Sage.

———. 1992. "International Relations Theory and Multilateralism: The Search for Foundations" *International Organization* 46 (Summer): 599–632.

Carlozzi, Nicholas, and John Taylor. 1985. "International Capital Mobility and the Coordination of Monetary Rules." In *Exchange Rate Management under Uncertainty,* edited by Jagdeep Bhandari, 186–211. MIT Press.

Carraro, Carlo, and Francesco Giavazzi. 1991. "Can International Policy Coordination Really be Counterproductive?" In *International Economic Policy Coordination,* edited by Carlo Carraro and others, 184–98. Oxford: Basil Blackwell.

Centre for Economic Policy Research. 1993. *Making Sense of Subsidiarity: How Much Centralization for Europe?* CEPR Annual Report on *Monitoring European Integration* 4. London.

Coase, Ronald H. 1960. "The Problem of Social Cost." *Journal of Law and Economics* 3 (October): 1–44.

Cohen, Benjamin J. 1990. "The Political Economy of International Trade." *International Organization* 44 (Spring): 261–81.

Collins, Susan M. Forthcoming. *Distributive Issues: A Constraint on Global Integration.* Brookings.

Cooper, Richard N. 1968. *The Economics of Interdependence: Economic Policy in the Atlantic Community.* McGraw-Hill.

———. 1969. "Macroeconomic Policy Adjustment in Interdependent Economies." *Quarterly Journal of Economics* 83 (February): 1–24.

———. 1974. "Worldwide Regional Integration: Is There an Optimal Size of the Integrated Area?" *Economic Notes* 3, 21–36. Siena: Monte dei Paschi di Siena.

———. 1984. "A Monetary System for the Future." *Foreign Affairs* 63 (Fall): 166–84.

———. 1986. "Economic Interdependence and Coordination of Economic Policies." In *Economic Policy in an Interdependent World,* edited by Richard N. Cooper, 289–331. MIT Press.

———. 1989. "International Cooperation in Public Health as a Prologue to Macroeconomic Cooperation." In *Can Nations Agree? Issues in International Economic Cooperation,* edited by Cooper and others, 178–254. Brookings.

———. 1990. "What Future for the International Monetary System?" In *The Evolution of the International Monetary System: How Can Efficiency and Stability*

Be Attained?, edited by Yoshio Suzuki, Junichi Miyake, and Mitsuake Okabe, 277–300. University of Tokyo Press.

———. 1994. *Environment and Resource Policies for the World Economy.* Brookings.

Corden, W. Max. 1983. "The Logic of the International Monetary Non-system." In *Reflections on a Troubled World Economy,* edited by Fritz Machlup, Gerhard Fels, and Hubertus Muller-Groeling, 59–74. St. Martin's Press.

———. 1986. "Fiscal Policies, Current Accounts and Real Exchange Rates: In Search of a Logic of International Policy Coordination," 423–38. *Weltwirtschaftliches Archiv,* Band 122, Heft 3.

———. 1994. *Economic Policy, Exchange Rates and the International System.* University of Chicago Press.

Crockett, Andrew. 1989. "The Role of International Institutions in Surveillance and Policy Coordination." In *Macroeconomic Policies in an Interdependent World,* edited by Ralph Bryant and others, 343–64. Brookings, Centre for Economic Policy Research, and International Monetary Fund.

Currie, David A., Gerald Holtham, and Andrew Hughes Hallett. 1989. "The Theory and Practice of International Policy Coordination: Does Coordination Pay?" In *Macroeconomic Policies in an Interdependent World,* edited by Ralph Bryant and others, 14–46. Brookings, Centre for Economic Policy Research, and International Monetary Fund.

Currie, David, and Paul Levine. 1985. "Macroeconomic Policy Design in an Interdependent World." In *International Economic Policy Coordination,* edited by Willem Buiter and Richard Marston, 228–68. Cambridge University Press.

Currie, David, Paul Levine, and Nic Vidalis. 1987. "International Cooperation and Reputation in an Empirical Two-Bloc Model." In *Global Macroeconomics: Policy Conflict and Cooperation,* edited by Ralph C. Bryant and Richard Portes, 75–121. London: Macmillan.

Currie, David A., and David Vines. 1988. *Macroeconomic Interactions between North and South.* Cambridge University Press.

Currie, David, and Simon Wren-Lewis. 1989a. "An Appraisal of Alternative Blueprints for International Policy Coordination." *European Economic Review* 33 (December): 1769–85.

———. 1989b. "Evaluating Blueprints for the Conduct of International Macro Policy." *American Economic Review* 79, *Papers and Proceedings* (May): 264–69.

———. 1990. "Evaluating the Extended Target-Zone Proposal for the G3." *Economic Journal* 100 (March): 105–23.

de Vries, Margaret Garritsen. 1976. *The International Monetary Fund, 1966–1971: The System under Stress.* Washington: International Monetary Fund.

Dobson, Wendy. 1991. *Economic Policy Coordination: Requiem or Prologue?*, Policy Analyses in International Economics 30. Washington: Institute for International Economics.

———. 1993. "Should G-7 Cooperation Be Buried?" *International Economic Insights* 4 (May-June):35–37.

———. 1994. "Economic Policy Coordination Institutionalized? The G-7 and the Future of the Bretton Woods Institution." In Bretton Woods Commission,

Bretton Woods: Looking to the Future, C143–48. Washington: Bretton Woods Commission.

Edison, Hali, Marcus H. Miller, and John Williamson. 1987. "On Evaluating and Extending the Target Zone Proposal." *Journal of Policy Modelling* 9 (Spring): 199–224.

Edison, Hali, and Ralph Tryon. 1988. "An Empirical Analysis of Policy Coordination in the United States, Japan, and Europe." In *Economic Modelling in the OECD Countries,* edited by Homa Motammen, 53–70. London: Chapman and Hall.

Eichengreen, Barry. 1992. *Should the Maastricht Treaty Be Saved?,* Princeton Studies in International Finance 74. Princeton University, International Finance Section (December).

———. 1993. "European Monetary Unification. " *Journal of Economic Literature* 31 (September): 1321–57.

———. 1994. *International Monetary Arrangements for the 21st Century.* Brookings.

Eichengreen, Barry, James Tobin, and Charles Wyplosz. 1995. "Two Cases for Sand in the Wheels of International Finance." *Economic Journal* 105 (January): 162–72.

Eichengreen, Barry, and Charles Wyplosz. 1993. "The Unstable EMS." *Brookings Papers on Economic Activity* 1: 51–143.

Elster, Jon. 1986. "The Market and the Forum: Three Varieties of Political Theory." In *Foundations of Social Choice Theory,* edited by Jon Elster and Aamund Hylland, 103–32. Cambridge University Press.

Emerson, Michael, and others. 1988. "The Economics of 1992." *European Economy* 38 (March).

Feldstein, Martin. 1988a. *International Economic Cooperation.* University of Chicago Press.

———. 1988b. "Distinguished Lecture on Economics in Government: Thinking about International Economic Cooperation." *Journal of Economic Perspectives* 2 (Spring): 3–13.

Fischer, Stanley. 1980. "Dynamic Inconsistency, Cooperation and the Benevolent Dissembling Government." In *Journal of Economic Dynamics and Control* 2 (February), 93–107.

———. 1988. "International Macroeconomic Policy Coordination." In *International Economic Cooperation,* edited by Martin Feldstein, 11–43. University of Chicago Press.

———. 1990a. "Rules versus Discretion in Monetary Policy." In *Handbook of Monetary Economics,* vol. 2, edited by B. M. Friedman and F. H. Hahn, 1155–84. Amsterdam: North-Holland.

———. 1990b. "Comment" on Peter Kenen, "The Coordination of Macroeconomic Policies." In *International Policy Coordination and Exchange Rate Fluctuations,* edited by William Branson and others, 105–08. University of Chicago Press.

———. 1994. "The Mission of the Fund." In Bretton Woods Commission, *Bretton Woods: Looking to the Future,* C161–70. Washington: Bretton Woods Commission.

Flood, Robert P., and Peter Isard. 1989. "Monetary Policy Strategies." *IMF Staff Papers* 36 (September): 612–32.

Frankel, Jeffrey A. 1988a. "Ambiguous Policy Multipliers in Theory and in Empirical Models." In *Empirical Macroeconomics for Interdependent Economies,* edited by Ralph C. Bryant and others, 17–26. Brookings.

———. 1988b. *Obstacles to International Macroeconomic Policy Coordination.* Princeton Studies in International Finance 64. Princeton, International Finance Section. Princeton University.

———. 1989. "Comment" on D. Currie, G. Holtham, and A. Hughes Hallett, "The Theory and Practice of International Policy Coordination: Does Coordination Pay?" In *Macroeconomic Policies in an Interdependent World,* edited by Ralph C. Bryant and others, 51–58. Brookings, Centre for Economic Policy Research, and International Monetary Fund.

———. 1990. "Obstacles to Coordination, and a Consideration of Two Proposals to Overcome Them: International Nominal Targeting (INT) and the Hosomi Fund." In *International Policy Coordination and Exchange Rate Fluctuations,* edited by William Branson and others, 109–45. University of Chicago Press.

Frankel, Jeffrey A., and Menzie Chinn. 1993. "The Stabilizing Properties of a Nominal GNP Rule in an Open Economy." Working Paper 259. University of California, Santa Cruz, Department of Economics (March).

Frankel, Jeffrey A., and Katharine E. Rockett. 1988. "International Macroeconomic Policy Coordination when Policymakers Do Not Agree on the True Model." *American Economic Review* 78 (June): 318–40.

Frankel, Jeffrey A., Scott Erwin, and Katharine Rockett. 1992. "International Macroeconomic Policy Coordination When Policymakers Do Not Agree on the True Model: Reply." *American Economic Review* 82 (September): 1052–56.

Frenkel, Jacob, Morris Goldstein, and Paul Masson. 1989. "Simulating the Effects of Some Simple Coordinated Versus Uncoordinated Policy Rules." In *Macroeconomic Policies in an Interdependent World,* edited by Ralph Bryant and others, 203–39. Brookings, Centre for Economic Policy Research, and International Monetary Fund.

———. 1990. "The Rationale for, and Effects of, International Economic Policy Coordination." In *International Policy Coordination and Exchange Rate Fluctuations,* edited by William Branson and others, 9–62. University of Chicago Press.

Friedman, Benjamin M. 1975. "Targets, Instruments, and Indicators of Monetary Policy." *Journal of Monetary Economics* 1 (October): 443–73.

———. 1990. "Targets and Instruments of Monetary Policy." In *Handbook of Monetary Economics,* vol. 2, edited by B. M. Friedman and F. H. Hahn, 1185–230. Amsterdam: North-Holland.

———. 1993. "The Role of Judgement and Discretion in the Conduct of Monetary Policy: Consequences of Changing Financial Markets." In *Changing Capital Markets: Implications for Monetary Policy,* 115–96. Symposium sponsored by the Federal Reserve Bank of Kansas City, Jackson Hole, Wyoming.

Frohlich, Norman, Joe A. Oppenheimer, and Oran R. Young. 1971. *Political Leadership and Collective Goods.* Princeton University Press.

Funabashi, Y. 1988. *Managing the Dollar: From the Plaza to the Louvre.* Washington: Institute for International Economics.

Gardner, Richard N. 1969. *Sterling-Dollar Diplomacy: The Origins and the Prospects of Our International Economic Order.* McGraw Hill.

Ghosh, Atish R. 1986. "International Policy Coordination in an Uncertain World." *Economics Letters* 21 (3): 271–76.

———. 1995. "International Capital Mobility Amongst the Major Industrialised Countries: Too Little or Too Much?" *Economic Journal* 105 (January): 107–28.

Ghosh, Atish R., and Swati R. Ghosh. 1991. "Does Model Uncertainty Really Preclude International Policy Coordination?" *Journal of International Economics* 31 (November): 325–40.

Ghosh, Atish R., and Paul R. Masson. 1988. "International Policy Coordination in a World with Model Uncertainty." *International Monetary Fund Staff Papers* 35 (June): 230–58.

———. 1991. "Model Uncertainty, Learning, and the Gains from Coordination." *American Economic Review* 81 (June): 465–79.

———. 1994. *Economic Cooperation in an Uncertain World.* Oxford: Basil Blackwell.

Giavazzi, Francesco, and Alberto Giovannini. 1989. *Limiting Exchange Rate Flexibility: The European Monetary System.* MIT Press.

Gilpin, Robert. 1975. *U.S. Power and the Multinational Corporation: The Political Economy of Foreign Direct Investment.* Basic Books.

Goldstein, Morris. 1992. "Improving Economic Policy Coordination: Evaluating Some New and Not-So-New Proposals." Paper prepared for Rinaldo Ossola Memorial Conference on the International Monetary System, Banca d'Italia.

———. 1995. "The Exchange Rate System and the IMF: A Modest Agenda." Washington: Institute for International Economics.

Goldstein, Morris, David Folkerts-Landau, Peter Garber, Liliana Rojas-Suarez, and Michael Spencer. 1993. *International Capital Markets, Part I. Exchange Rate Management and International Capital Flows.* Washington: International Monetary Fund.

Goldstein, Morris, and Peter Isard. 1992. "Mechanisms for Promoting Global Monetary Stability." In *Policy Issues in the Evolving International Monetary System,* edited by Morris Goldstein and others, 1–36. Occasional Paper 96. Washington: International Monetary Fund (June).

Gordon, Roger H. 1983. "An Optimal Taxation Approach to Fiscal Federalism." *Quarterly Journal of Economics* 98 (November): 567–86.

Group of Thirty. 1988. *International Macroeconomic Policy Coordination.* New York: Group of Thirty.

Grunberg, Isabelle. 1990. "Exploring the 'Myth' of Hegemonic Stability." *International Organization* 44 (Autumn): 431–77.

Haas, Ernst B. 1980. "Why Colloborate? Issue-Linkage and International Regimes." *World Politics* 32 (April): 357–405.

———. 1983. "Words Can Hurt You: Or Who Said What to Whom about Regimes." In *International Regimes,* edited by Stephen D. Krasner, 23–59. Cornell University Press.

Haas, Peter M. 1990. *Saving the Mediterranean: The Politics of International Environmental Cooperation.* Columbia University Press.

———. 1992a. "Introduction: Epistemic Communities and International Policy Coordination," *International Organization* 46, special issue on Knowledge, Power, and International Policy Coordination (Winter): 1–35.

———. 1992b. "Banning Chlorofluorocarbons: Epistemic Community Efforts to Protect Stratospheric Ozone." *International Organization* 46, special issue on Knowledge, Power, and International Policy Coordination (Winter): 187–224.

Haggard, Stephan. 1995. *Developing Nations and the Politics of Global Integration.* Brookings.

Haggard, Stephan, and Beth A. Simmons. 1987. "Theories of International Regimes." *International Organization* 41 (Summer): 491–517.

Halperin, Morton H., with Priscilla Clapp and Arnold Kanter. 1974. *Bureaucratic Politics and Foreign Policy.* Brookings.

Hamada, Koichi. 1974. "Alternative Exchange Rate Systems and the Interdependence of Monetary Policies." In *National Monetary Policies and the International Financial System,* edited by Robert Aliber, 13–33. University of Chicago Press.

———. 1976. "A Strategic Analysis of Monetary Interdependence." *Journal of Political Economy* 84 (August): 677–700.

———. 1977. "On the Political Economy of Monetary Integration: A Public Economics Approach." In *The Political Economy of Monetary Reform,* edited by Robert Z. Aliber, 13–31. Macmillan.

———. 1979. "Macroeconomic Strategy and Coordination under Alternative Exchange Rates." In *International Economic Policy: Theory and Evidence,* edited by Rudiger Dornbusch and Jacob Frenkel, 292–324. Johns Hopkins University Press.

———. 1985. *The Political Economy of International Monetary Interdependence.* MIT Press.

———. 1986. "Strategic Aspects of International Fiscal Interdependence." *Economic Studies Quarterly* 37 (June): 165–80.

Hardin, Russell. 1982. *Collective Action.* Johns Hopkins University Press.

Helliwell, John F. 1988. "The Effects of Fiscal Policy on International Imbalances: Japan and the United States." Working Paper 2650. Cambridge, Mass.: National Bureau of Economic Research (July).

Helliwell, John F., Jon Cockerline, and Robert Lafrance. 1988. "Multicountry Modelling of Financial Markets." Working Paper 2736. Cambridge, Mass.: National Bureau of Economic Research (October).

Herring, Richard J., and Robert E. Litan. 1995. *Financial Regulation in the Global Economy.* Brookings.

Hirsch, Fred. 1976. *Social Limits to Growth.* Harvard University Press.

Hirschman, Albert O. 1970. *Exit, Voice, and Loyalty: Responses to Decline in Firms, Organizations, and States.* Harvard University Press.

Holtham, Gerald. 1986. "International Policy Co-ordination: How Much Consensus Is There?" Discussion Paper in International Economics 56. Brookings (September).

————. 1989a. "German Macroeconomic Policy and the 1978 Bonn Economic Summit." In *Can Nations Agree? Issues in International Economic Cooperation,* edited by Richard N. Cooper and others, 141–77. Brookings.

————. 1989b. "Foreign Exchange Markets and Target Zones." *Oxford Review of Economic Policy* 5 (Autumn): 73–82.

Holtham, Gerald, and Andrew Hughes Hallett. 1987. "International Policy Cooperation and Model Uncertainty." In *Global Macroeconomics: Policy Conflict and Cooperation,* edited by R. Bryant and R. Portes, 128–77. London: Macmillan.

————. 1992. "International Macroeconomic Policy Coordination When Policymakers Do Not Agree on the True Model: Comment." *American Economic Review* 82 (September): 1043–51.

Hooper, Peter, and others, eds., 1990. *Financial Sectors in Open Economies: Empirical Analysis and Policy Issues.* Washington: Board of Governors of the Federal Reserve System.

Horne, Jocelyn, and Paul Masson. 1988. "Scope and Limits of International Economic Cooperation and Policy Coordination." *International Monetary Fund Staff Papers* 35 (June): 259–96.

Horsefield, J. Keith. 1969. *The International Monetary Fund, 1945–1965.* Washington: International Monetary Fund.

Hughes Hallett, Andrew. 1986a. "Autonomy and the Choice of Policy in Asymmetrically Dependent Economies: An Investigation of the Gains from International Policy Coordination." *Oxford Economic Papers* 38 (November): 516–44.

————. 1986b. "International Policy Design and the Sustainability of Policy Bargains." *Journal of Economic Dynamics and Control* 10 (December): 467–94.

————. 1987. "The Impact of Interdependence on Economic Policy Design: The Case of the US, EEC and Japan." *Economic Modelling* 4 (July): 377–96.

————. 1989. "What Are the Risks in Coordinating Economic Policies Internationally?" In *Exchange Rates and Open Economy Macroeconomics,* edited by R. MacDonald and M. Taylor, 307–41. Oxford: Basil Blackwell.

————. 1992. "Target Zones and International Policy Coordination: The Contrast between the Necessary and Sufficient Conditions for Success." *European Economic Review* 36 (May): 893–914.

————. 1993. "Exchange Rates and Asymmetric Policy Regimes: When Does Exchange Rate Targeting Pay?" *Oxford Economic Papers* 45 (April): 191–206.

Hughes Hallett, Andrew, Gerald Holtham, and Gary Hutson. 1989. "Exchange Rate Targeting as Surrogate International Cooperation." In *Blueprints for Exchange Rate Management,* edited by B. Eichengreen, M. Miller, and R. Portes, 239–78. Academic Press.

Ikenberry, G. John. 1993. "Salvaging the G-7." *Foreign Affairs* 72 (Spring): 132–39.

Kahler, Miles. 1992. "Multilateralism with Small and Large Numbers." *International Organization* 46 (Summer): 681–708.

————. 1995. *International Institutions and the Political Economy of Integration.* Brookings.

Kahn, Alfred E. 1966. "The Tyranny of Small Decisions: Market Failures, Imperfections, and the Limits of Economics." *Kyklos* 19 (2): 23–47.

Kanbur, Ravi, and Michael Keen. 1993. "Jeux Sans Frontieres: Tax Competition and Tax Coordination When Countries Differ in Size." *American Economic Review* 83 (September): 877–92.

Kareken, John H., Thomas Muench, and Neil Wallace. 1973. "Optimal Open Market Strategy: The Use of Information Variables." *American Economic Review* 63 (March): 156–72.

Katzenstein, Peter J., ed. 1978. *Between Power and Plenty: Foreign Economic Policies of Advanced Industrial States.* University of Wisconsin Press.

Kehoe, Patrick. 1986. "International Policy Cooperation May Be Undesirable." Federal Reserve Bank of Minneapolis Staff Reports 103. Federal Reserve Bank of Minneapolis (February).

———. 1989. "Policy Cooperation among Benevolent Governments May Be Undesirable." *Review of Economic Studies* 56 (April): 289–96.

Kenen, Peter B. 1989. *Exchange Rates and Policy Coordination.* University of Michigan Press.

———. 1990. "The Coordination of Macroeconomic Policies." In *International Policy Coordination and Exchange Rate Fluctuations,* edited by William Branson and others, 63–108. University of Chicago Press.

———. 1992. *EMU After Maastricht.* Washington: Group of Thirty.

Keohane, Robert O. 1980. "The Theory of Hegemonic Stability and Changes in International Economic Regimes." In *Change in the International System,* edited by Ole R. Holsti, Randolph M. Siverson, and Alexander L. George, 131–62. Westview Press.

———. 1983. "The Demand for International Regimes." In *International Regimes,* edited by Stephen D. Krasner, 141–71. Cornell University Press.

———. 1984. *After Hegemony: Cooperation and Discord in the World Political Economy.* Princeton University Press.

———. 1986. "Reciprocity in International Relations," *International Organization* 40 (Winter): 1–27.

———. 1988. "International Institutions: Two Approaches." *International Studies Quarterly* 32 (December): 379–96.

Keohane, Robert O., and Joseph S. Nye. 1977. *Power and Interdependence: World Politics in Transition.* Little, Brown.

Kindleberger, Charles P. 1973. *The World in Depression, 1929–1939.* University of California Press.

———. 1986. "International Public Goods without International Government." *American Economic Review* 76 (March): 1–13.

Krasner, Stephen D., ed. 1983a. *International Regimes.* Cornell University Press.

Krasner, Stephen D. 1983b. "Structural Causes and Regime Consequences." In *International Regimes,* edited by Stephen D. Krasner, 1–21. Cornell University Press.

——— 1983c. "Regimes and the Limits of Realism: Regimes as Autonomous Variables," In *International Regimes,* edited by Stephen D. Krasner, 355–68. Cornell University Press.

Kreps, David, and others. 1982. "Rational Cooperation in the Finitely Repeated Prisoners Dilemma." *Journal of Economic Theory* 27 (August): 245–52.

Kreps, David, and Robert Wilson, 1982. "Reputation and Imperfect Information." *Journal of Economic Theory* 27 (August): 253–79.

Krueger, Anne O. 1995. *Trade Policies and Developing Nations.* Brookings.

Kydland, Finn, and Edward Prescott. 1977. "Rules Rather than Discretion: The Inconsistency of Optimal Plans." *Journal of Political Economy* 85 (June): 473–91.

Lawrence, Robert Z. Forthcoming. *Regionalism, Multilateralism, and Deeper Integration.* Brookings.

Levine, Paul, and David Currie. 1987. "Does International Macroeconomic Policy Coordination Pay and Is It Sustainable?: A Two Country Analysis." *Oxford Economic Papers* 39 (March): 38–74.

Levine, Paul, David A. Currie, and Jessica Gaines. 1989. "The Use of Simple Rules for International Policy Agreements." In *Blueprints for Exchange Rate Management,* edited by Barry Eichengreen, Marcus Miller, and Richard Portes, 281–319. Academic Press.

March, James G., and Johan P. Olsen. 1984. "The New Institutionalism: Organizational Factors in Political Life," *American Political Science Review* 78 (September): 734–49.

March, James G., and Herbert A. Simon. 1958. *Organizations.* John Wiley and Sons.

Masson, Paul R. 1992. "Portfolio Preference Uncertainty and Gains from Policy Coordination." *IMF Staff Papers* 39 (March): 101–20.

———. 1994. "The Credibility of the United Kingdom's Commitment to the ERM: Intentions versus Actions." IMF Working Paper WP/94/147. Washington: International Monetary Fund.

———. 1995. "Gaining and Losing ERM Credibility: The Case of the United Kingdom." *Economic Journal* 105 (May): 571–82.

McCallum, Bennett T. 1985. "On Consequences and Criticisms of Monetary Targeting." *Journal of Money, Credit, and Banking* 17 (November): 570–97.

———. 1990. "Targets, Indicators, and Instruments of Monetary Policy." In *Monetary Policy for a Changing Financial Environment,* edited by William S. Haraf and Phillip Cagan, 44–70. Washington: American Enterprise Institute for Public Policy Research.

McGuire, Martin. 1974. "Group Segregation and Optimal Jurisdictions." *Journal of Political Economy* 82 (January-February): 112–32.

McKibbin, Warwick J. 1988. "The Economics of International Policy Coordination." *Economic Record* 64 (December): 241–53.

McKibbin, Warwick J., and Jeffrey D. Sachs. 1988. "Coordination of Monetary and Fiscal Policies in the Industrial Economies." In *International Aspects of Fiscal Policies,* edited by Jacob A. Frenkel, 73–113. University of Chicago Press for the National Bureau of Economic Research.

———. 1989. "Implications of Policy Rules for the World Economy." In *Macroeconomic Policies in an Interdependent World,* edited by Ralph C. Bryant and others, 151–94. Brookings.

———. 1991. *Global Linkages: Macroeconomic Interdependence and Cooperation in the World Economy.* Brookings.

McKinnon, Ronald I. 1984. *An International Standard for Monetary Stabilization,* Policy Analyses in International Economics 8. Washington: Institute for International Economics (March).

———. 1988. "Monetary and Exchange Rate Policies for International Financial Stability: A Proposal." *Journal of Economic Perspectives* 2 (Winter): 83–103.

Meade, James E. 1952. "External Economies and Diseconomies in a Competitive Situation." *Economic Journal* 62 (March 1952): 54–67.

Miller, Marcus, and Mark Salmon. 1985. "Policy Coordination and Dynamic Games." In *International Economic Policy Coordination,* edited by Willem H. Buiter and Richard C. Marston, 184–213. Cambridge University Press.

Møller, J. Ørstrøm. 1995. *The Future European Model: Economic Internationalization and Cultural Decentralization.* Praeger.

Nayar, Baldev Ray. 1995. "Regimes, Power, and International Aviation." *International Organization* 49 (Winter): 139–70.

Nedde, Ellen Marie. 1989. "Dynamic Gains to Strategic Policy-Making and International Economic Policy Coordination." Ph.D. dissertation, University of Maryland.

Niehans, Jurg. 1968. "Monetary and Fiscal Policies in Open Economies Under Fixed Exchange Rates: An Optimizing Approach." *Journal of Political Economy* 76 (July-August): 893–920.

Oakland, William H. 1987. "Theory of Public Goods." In *Handbook of Public Economics,* vol. 2, edited by Alan J. Auerbach and Martin Feldstein, 485–535. Amsterdam: North-Holland.

Oates, Wallace E. 1972. *Fiscal Federalism.* Harcourt, Brace, Jovanovich.

———, ed. 1977. *The Political Economy of Fiscal Federalism.* Lexington Books.

———. 1985. "Searching for Leviathan: An Empirical Study." *American Economic Review* 75 (September): 748–57.

Olson, Mancur. 1969. "The Principle of 'Fiscal Equivalence': The Division of Responsibilities Among Different Levels of Government." *American Economic Review* 59, *Papers and Proceedings* (May): 479–87.

———. 1971. *The Logic of Collective Action: Public Goods and the Theory of Groups,* 2d ed. Harvard University Press.

Oudiz, Gilles, and Jeffrey Sachs. 1984. "Macroeconomic Policy Coordination among the Industrial Economies." *Brookings Papers on Economic Activity* 1: 1–64.

———. 1985. "International Policy Coordination in Dynamic Macroeconomic Models." In *International Economic Policy Coordination,* edited by Willem H. Buiter and Richard C. Marston, 274–319. Cambridge University Press.

Paarlberg, Robert L. 1995. *Leadership Abroad Begins at Home: U.S. Foreign Economic Policy after the Cold War.* Brookings.

Pauly, Louis W. 1992. "The Political Foundations of Multilateral Economic Surveillance." *International Journal* 47 (Spring): 293–327.

Peters, B. Guy. 1992. "Bureaucratic Politics and the Institutions of the European Community." In *Euro-Politics: Institutions and Policymaking in the 'New' European Community,* edited by Alberta M. Sbragia, 75–122. Brookings.

Peterson, Paul E. 1995. *The Price of Federalism.* Brookings.

Polak, Jacques J. 1981. *Coordination of National Economic Policies*, Group of Thirty Occasional Paper 7. New York: Group of Thirty.

———. 1991. "International Policy Coordination and the Functioning of the International Monetary System." In *The Reality of International Economic Policy Coordination*, edited by H. J. Blommestein, 151–71. Amsterdam: North Holland.

Powell, Walter W., and Paul J. DiMaggio, eds. 1991. *The New Institutionalism in Organizational Analysis*. University of Chicago Press.

Putnam, Robert D. 1988. "Diplomacy and Domestic Politics: The Logic of Two-Level Games. *International Organization* 42 (Summer): 427–60.

Putnam, Robert D., and Nicholas Bayne. 1984. *Hanging Together: The Seven-Power Summits*. Harvard University Press.

Putnam, Robert D., and C. Randall Henning. 1989. "The Bonn Summit of 1978: A Case Study in Coordination." In *Can Nations Agree? Issues in International Economic Cooperation*, edited by Richard N. Cooper and others, 12–140. Brookings.

Rapoport, Anatol. 1960. *Fights, Games, and Debates*. University of Michigan Press.

Rogoff, Kenneth. 1985a. "Can International Monetary Policy Cooperation Be Counterproductive?" *Journal of International Economics* 18 (May): 199–217.

———. 1985b. "The Optimal Degree of Commitment to an Intermediate Monetary Target." *Quarterly Journal of Economics* 100 (November): 1169–89.

———. 1987. "Reputational Constraints on Monetary Policy." In *Bubbles and Other Essays*, edited by Karl Brunner and Allan Meltzer, 141–81. *Carnegie-Rochester Conference Series on Public Policy*, vol. 26. Amsterdam: North-Holland.

Rubinfeld, Daniel L. 1987. "The Economics of the Local Public Sector." In *Handbook of Public Economics*, vol. 2, edited by Alan J. Auerbach and Martin Feldstein, 571–645. Amsterdam: North-Holland.

Ruggie, John Gerard. 1975. "International Responses to Technology: Concepts and Trends." *International Organization* 29 (Summer): 557–83.

———. 1983. "International Regimes, Transactions, and Change: Embedded Liberalism in the Postwar Economic Order." In *International Regimes*, edited by Stephen D. Krasner, 195–231. Cornell University Press.

———. 1992. "Multilateralism: The Anatomy of an Institution." *International Organization* 46 (Summer): 561–98.

Sbragia, Alberta M., ed. 1992a. *Euro-Politics: Institutions and Policymaking in the 'New' European Community*. Brookings.

Sbragia, Alberta M. 1992b. "Thinking about the European Future: The Uses of Comparison." In *Euro-Politics: Institutions and Policymaking in the 'New' European Community*, edited by Alberta M. Sbragia, 257–91. Brookings.

Schelling, Thomas. 1974. "On the Ecology of Micromotives." In *The Corporate Society*, edited by Robin Marris, 19–64. Wiley.

———. 1978. *Micromotives and Macrobehavior*. Norton.

Scitovsky, Tibor. 1954. "Two Concepts of External Economies." *Journal of Political Economy* 62 (April): 143–51.

Sebenius, James K. 1992. "Challenging Conventional Explanations of International Cooperation: Negotiation Analysis and the Case of Epistemic Communities." *International Organization* 46 (Winter): 323–66.

Simon, Herbert A. 1959. "Theories of Decision-Making in Economics and Behavioral Science." *American Economic Review* 49 (June): 253–83.

Sinn, Hans-Werner. 1990. "Tax Harmonization and Tax Competition in Europe." *European Economic Review* 34 (May): 489–504.

Snidal, Duncan. 1985. "The Limits of Hegemonic Stability Theory," *International Organization* 39 (Autumn): 579–614.

Solomon, Robert. 1982. *The International Monetary System, 1945–1981.* Harper and Row.

———. 1991. "Background Paper." In *Partners in Prosperity: The Report of the Twentieth Century Fund Task Force on the International Coordination of National Economic Policies,* 45–124. Priority Press Publications.

———. 1994. *The Transformation of the World Economy, 1980–93.* London: Macmillan.

Stein, Arthur A. 1983. "Coordination and Collaboration: Regimes in an Anarchic World." In *International Regimes,* edited by Stephen D. Krasner, 115–40. Cornell University Press.

Stein, Herbert. 1978. "International Coordination of Domestic Economic Policies." *AEI Economist* (June): 1–6.

———. 1987. "International Coordination of Economic Policy." *AEI Economist* (August): 1–7.

Steinbruner, John D. 1974. *The Cybernetic Theory of Decision: New Dimensions of Political Analysis.* Princeton University Press.

Strange, Susan. 1983. *"Cave! Hic Dragones: A Critique of Regime Analysis."* In *International Regimes,* edited by Stephen D. Krasner, 337–354. Cornell University Press.

Sykes, Alan O. 1995. *Product Standards for Internationally Integrated Goods Markets.* Brookings.

Tabellini, Guido. 1988. "Domestic Politics and the International Coordination of Fiscal Policies." CEPR Working Paper 226. London: Centre for Economic Policy Research (January).

Tanzi, Vito. 1989. "International Coordination of Fiscal Policies: Current and Future Issues." In *Fiscal Policy, Economic Adjustment, and Financial Markets,* edited by Mario Monti, 7–37. Washington: International Monetary Fund.

Tanzi, Vito. 1995. *Taxation in an Integrating World.* Brookings.

Taylor, John B. 1985. "International Coordination in the Design of Macroeconomic Policy Rules." *European Economic Review* 28 (June–July): 53–81.

———. 1988. "The Treatment of Expectations in Large Multicountry Econometric Models." In *Empirical Macroeconomics for Interdependent Economies,* edited by Ralph C. Bryant and others, 161–82. Brookings.

———. 1989. "Policy Analysis with a Multicountry Model," In *Macroeconomic Policies in an Interdependent World,* edited by Ralph Bryant and others, 122–41. Washington: International Monetary Fund.

Taylor, Michael. 1987. *The Possibility of Cooperation.* Cambridge University Press.

Turnovsky, Stephen, and Vasco d'Orey. 1986. "Monetary Policies in Interdependent Economies with Stochastic Disturbances: A Strategic Approach." *Economic Journal* 96 (September): 696–721.

Turnovsky, Stephen, Tamer Basar, and Vasco d'Orey. 1988. "Dynamic Strategic Monetary Policies and Coordination in Interdependent Economies." *American Economic Review* 78 (June): 341–61.

van-der-Ploeg, Fredrick. 1988. "International Policy Coordination in Interdependent Monetary Economics." *Journal of International Economics* 25 (August): 1–23.

Vaubel, Roland. 1983. "Coordination or Competition Among National Macroeconomic Policies?" In *Reflections on a Troubled World Economy: Essays in Honor of Herbert Giersch,* edited by F. Machlup, G. Fels, and H. Muller-Groeling, 3–28. London: St. Martin's Press.

———. 1985. "International Collusion or Competition for Macroeconomic Policy Coordination? A Restatement." *Recherches Economiques de Louvain* 51 (December): 223–40.

Wallace, William. 1994. *Regional Integration: The West European Experience.* Brookings.

Waltz, Kenneth. 1979. *Theory of International Politics.* Addison-Wesley.

Waud, Roger N. 1973. "Proximate Targets and Monetary Policy." *Economic Journal* 83 (March): 1–20.

Williamson, John. 1977. *The Failure of World Monetary Reform, 1971–74.* New York University Press.

———. 1991. "FEERs and the ERM." *National Institute Economic Review* 137 (August): 45–50.

———. 1993. "Exchange Rate Management." *Economic Journal* 103 (January): 188–97.

Williamson, John, ed. 1994. *Estimating Equilibrium Exchange Rates.* Washington: Institute for International Economics.

Williamson, John, and C. Randall Henning. 1994. "Managing the Monetary System." In *Managing the World Economy: Fifty Years after Bretton Woods,* edited by Peter B. Kenen, C83–111. Washington: Institute for International Economics.

Williamson, John, and Marcus Miller. 1987. *Targets and Indicators: A Blueprint for the International Coordination of Economic Policy.* Policy Analyses in International Economics 22. Washington: Institute for International Economics.

Wilson, John D. 1986. "A Theory of Interregional Tax Competition," *Journal of Urban Economics* 19 (May): 296–315.

Working Group on Exchange Market Intervention. 1983. *Report of the Working Group on Exchange Market Intervention.* Paris: Documentation Francaise.

Young, Oran R. 1986. "International Regimes: Toward a New Theory of Institutions." *World Politics* 39 (October): 104–22.

———. 1989a. "The Politics of International Regime Formation: Managing Natural Resources and the Environment." *International Organization* 43 (Summer): 349–75.

———. 1989b. *International Cooperation: Building Regimes for Natural Resources and the Environment.* Cornell University Press.

———. 1991. "Political Leadership and Regime Formation: On the Development of Institutions in International Society." *International Organization* 45 (Summer 1991): 281–308.

Index

157